BUILDINGS FOR MODEL RAILWAYS

Maurice H. Bradley, ARIBA
Chartered Architect

DAVID & CHARLES
Newton Abbot London North Pomfret (VT)

To my wife for her unfailing support
and encouragement

British Library Cataloguing In Publication Data

Bradley, Maurice H.
    Buildings for model railways
    1. Railways—Models   2. Architectural models
    I. Title
    625.1'9   TF197

ISBN 0–7153–8343–4

Typeset by Photo-Graphics, Honiton, Devon
and printed in Great Britain
by Biddles Limited, Guildford, Surrey
for David & Charles (Publishers) Limited
Brunel House Newton Abbot Devon

Published in the United States of America
by David & Charles Inc
North Pomfret Vermont 05053 USA

Contents

Introduction

As a railway modeller for over 30 years, when I eventually became interested in creating a complete environment for the layout, it was to the late John Ahern's *Miniature Building Construction* that I turned for guidance. Although written in the closing years of the second world war, many of his techniques and methods hold good today and it is as a continuation of the ideas first promulgated by him, that I developed the ideas and practices for this book. Materials and methods change with the passing years, and the coming of plastics together with vastly improved adhesives, chemical etching, modelling pastes, colours and transfers, have revolutionized the modelling scene. In addition, the present day modeller has at his command a whole range of miniature power tools which immeasurably increase the scope of his operations and the standard of finish.

The quality of ready to run railway models, both locomotives and rolling stock, generally is now at so high a level that for what is virtually the price of a toy, one can obtain a scale model of such fidelity to the prototype that in a photograph, the one is often mistaken for the other. It seems a pity therefore, if we cannot make an attempt to haul the rest of the layout into the same standards.

Of course a large range of plastic kits for miniature buildings is readily available but for the most part they are of continental prototypes and to a scale not entirely compatible with the average British layout. The sight of a miniature Cornish Riviera Express passing through a landscape more typical of the Bavarian Alps, apart from being visually confusing, detracts from the quality of the models and reduces the whole layout to the status of a toy.

Over the past few years I have written a number of articles for the specialist model railway magazines on a variety of topics, but mainly concerned with model building construction and a little while ago Chris Ellis, Editor of *Model Trains* suggested that it would be a good idea to produce a series of articles on the modelling techniques involved in using modern materials. It is from his suggestion that the present work has developed. Some of the illustrations and drawings have appeared previously in the pages of *Model Trains*, *Railway Modeller*, *Model Railways* and *Model Railway Constructor* but most of the present material has been prepared specially for this book. While written primarily for the model railway enthusiast and thereby due emphasis has been placed on railway structures, nevertheless it is hoped that the appeal will be wider and include diorama modellers and architectural modellers of all types from those studying architecture and building construction for examination purposes to the student architect.

Skill in modelling is a commercial asset and the gifted amateur can turn his ability to financial advantage in preparing models for display, for builders and contractors, building societies and estate agents, architects and engineers and in many other fields, apart from the satisfaction of creating the models for their own sake. A good model is a work of art in three dimensions and unlike a drawing, can be studied from many angles and in a variety of settings.

Those who have visited Pendon Museum and seen the exquisite work in the construction of 'Pendon Parva' and the associated 4mm scale model railway will need no words of mine to convince them of the heights to which scenic modelling can aspire. At its simplest level, it can provide a convincing, true to scale and period setting for a model railway layout; at its most inspired, it can present a finished picture so convincing that it requires almost an effort of will to assure oneself that one is not looking at reality, albeit through a reducing glass.

Of course work of this quality infers a considerable degree of skill in its execution, a skill which the beginner may often feel is well beyond his capabilities. But like everything else, practice leads to perfection and you will be surprised how rapidly you progress in the art until you find that you are actively seeking out unusual and difficult prototypes to model. As in all creative work, the most difficult part of the whole operation is to make a start!

Maurice H. Bradley
Exeter

Mediaeval and Georgian often go together in towns where modern developers have not done their worst. They are an ideal prototype for a railway in a country town setting.

1
Subjects to Model

Obtaining and Recording Information

One of the problems in the preparation of a book on architectural modelling lies in the presentation of the plans and in particular, the scale to be used. For the 4mm modeller who undoubtedly is in the majority at least as far as the UK is concerned, the ideal solution would be to include the plans full size for that scale. Unfortunately this would have led to a page size which from the Publisher's point of view would be completely uneconomical. To overcome this problem, a drawn scale is included with each of the plans and should you wish to work from one of these drawings, you will find that it is a simple matter to have the plan either enlarged or reduced to any required scale by your local Copy Shop. Most Local Authorities, either District or County Councils, also maintain a well equipped copying department and for a nominal sum will usually provide a similar service. It simply is not worth attempting to save the small cost involved by re-drawing the plans yourself. You will of course, find the work much easier and quicker if you model direct from a drawing to the correct scale.

Incidentally all the plans included have been used in the preparation of model structures and if you follow them absolutely literally (subject to making due allowance for the thickness of any material you use) you will finish up with an accurate copy. To simplify the work, wherever necessary I have endeavoured to include extended elevations of bay windows and the like so that in the preparation of the general fenestration, the sashes and glazing bars may be traced directly from the drawing.

Undoubtedly in the course of your modelling career you will wish to construct a model of a building or buildings for which scale drawings are not readily available and it will be useful to pause for a moment to consider the sources of information open to the modeller.

Railway Structures, Stations, Goods Depots, Signalboxes and the like

Photographs and drawings of a very wide range of buildings may be obtained from the BR/OPC Joint Drawings Scheme of 302, Holdenhurst Road, Bournemouth, Dorset. In addition the British Rail District Civil Engineer of the area in which you are interested may be approached (see telephone directory) and these gentlemen can prove to be a mine of information.

The Ordnance Survey can also be very helpful, particularly in the provision of station layouts and it is worth remembering that they keep on file survey maps dating back for 80 to 100 years which can be of considerable assistance to those modelling period layouts.

General photographs are also very useful and the well known Locomotive & General Railway Photographs collection owned by David & Charles Ltd, the publisher of this book, are available through Real Photographs, Terminal House, Shepperton, Middlesex.

The various publishing houses specialising in railway matters cover a very wide spectrum indeed and a few hours' research in this field can prove rewarding. Between them they have published a mass of accurate and valuable information and before undertaking the time consuming exercise of a personal survey, it is well worth finding out whether someone has been there before you and has published the results of his investigations!

Before leaving this section, I would like to mention the various County reference libraries which keep in their store rooms an amazing collection of historical information. Many local authorities file their deposited plans with the County Archivist after the expiry of 15 or 20 years and it is perfectly possible to turn up the original working drawings associated with branch lines which faded from view long before the Beeching Axe was swung.

Commercial Premises, Shops, Warehouses, etc

You will often find that a courteous approach to the company or individual occupying the premises in which you are interested, will yield a handsome dividend and very often results in a copy of the architect's plans particularly if

The country town station with its variety of architectural styles.

The Maltings set out in Figures 32 and 33.

The 'Dutch' House shown in Figure 28.

recent works of modernisation or modification have been carried out. This comment applies with particular force to premises owned or occupied by the larger multiple or national companies who in most cases have their own architects' departments and are usually most helpful to the amateur modeller. Remember also that it costs very little and does much for the public image of the hobby if on completion of the model you let the owner of the premises have a photograph of your work.

Private Premises, Dwelling Houses, etc

The old maxim 'do unto others as you yourself would be done by' is particularly relevant to this type of work. When making any sketches or taking dimensions, it goes without saying that the occupier or owner should be approached and permission received before proceeding. You will very often find that the owner with no prompting whatever, can turn up old photographs and drawings which can be invaluable to you in your work. It is usual to repay any such kindness by letting the owner have copies of any sketches or photographs you may make, and a photograph of the completed model is always well received.

Finally it is worth remembering that the local authority, usually the District Council, keeps on file a large number of deposited plans until they find a final resting place with the County Archivist. An approach to the Planning or Building Regulations Departments can often turn up information which would be difficult to obtain in any other way. The officials concerned will, however, require to know the purpose for which you wish to inspect the drawings and it is usual to have the building owner's written permission before proceeding with this line of investigation.

Before deciding on the final and most accurate method of recording an existing building, namely a measured survey, it is worth considering the feasibility of preparing a set of drawings from site photographs. Assuming you have a companion of known height, it is a simple matter to position him or her against the elevation being recorded before taking the photograph. Try to take the various exposures as square on to the building as possible so that perspective complications do not cause difficulty. It is then a relatively simple matter to convert your photographs into a set of scale drawings using the height of your companion to provide a scale on the photographs themselves. It pays dividends also to enlarge the prints to at least 7in × 5in or thereabouts and on matt paper so that you can sketch over them in pencil as required.

Figure 1 explains the method which is based on a photograph (one of several) of the Passage Inn at Topsham, from which the model which is dealt with in more detail in a later chapter, was made.

Unfortunately due to the restricted width of the roadway, it proved impossible to take a photograph absolutely square on to the building, so a certain amount of work was required to modify the effect of perspective on the dimensions.

I had asked my wife (who is 5ft 10in tall to the top of her sun hat) to stand as close as possible to the near corner of the Inn. On the sketch I then projected a line from the top of her hat and another from her feet to this corner, used as a datum on the photograph (line AA). Using any convenient scale and slanting the rule as necessary to divide my wife's height into 5ft 10in exactly, it was then a relatively simple matter using dividers, to draw an accurate scale of feet along the datum line, and this you can see along line AA. For convenience I extended this scale to the right hand margin of the drawing to disentangle it so to speak from the detail of the photograph.

As the front elevation of the Inn is in slightly diminishing perspective, you will see that it is necessary to project the height of such details as doors and windows onto the datum line to arrive at their true height. For example XY indicates the height of the small sash window over the entrance door. This height is extended (following the true perspective of head and cill) onto datum line AA from which it can be seen that the cill height above ground base of datum is 8ft 5in and the total height of the window 4ft 0in or thereabouts.

With regard to lengths on plan, when taking the photographs it pays to make a note of rough overall dimensions from the salient angles of the building, and with practice this can be paced out with reasonable accuracy. It provides an additional check on the dimensions deduced from the photographs.

Although absolute accuracy is not possible utilizing this method, nevertheless you will be

Figure 1   SCALING   FROM   PHOTOGRAPHS

surprised how close you can get and in circumstances where it is quite impossible to measure the building concerned later (it may perhaps have been demolished) it provides a method of preparing a reasonable set of drawings from photographs sufficient at least to capture the character of the building.

As an additional aid, I invariably carry a folding 6ft 0in rod in the car and to be truthful this represents the sum total of my surveying equipment. It is very handy to note spot dimensions where a full survey is not anticipated, it can be stood against a building and photographed alongside any complicated details (column caps, bases, moulded quoins and so on) when it gives a ready check on dimensions and at a push it can be used as a makeshift theodolite to assess the heights of buildings and perhaps trees where this is not possible by any other means. A folding rod of this type dimensioned either in feet and inches or centimetres and metres can be purchased at any drawing supplies shop and will be found invaluable, much more so than a Surveyor's tape which besides being considerably more expensive, requires the use of an assistant who is often not available

when most required.

Before leaving the prototype of a potential model it pays to make a note in your record book of the followings details:

(a) Finish and colour of materials of external walls, ie, whether brick (type and size), stucco, stone, (ashlar, rubble, coursed rubble, squared and snecked) weatherboarding, tile hanging and so on. If the building is in faced brickwork, apart from noting the size of the brick, measure the height of four courses and four bed joints. This will give you a very accurate guide to heights when taking dimensions from a photograph.

(b) Type of windows and materials used – vertical sliding, sash, casements (timber or steel), Yorkshire lights (horizontal sliders).

(c) Type of doors, four- or six-panelled, ledged and braced, studded and so on. Apart from the pattern of windows and doors, the character of a building is very much influenced by the depth of reveals to the openings generally. Although such details may be readily picked up

Above: Record sketch of cottage architecture.

Left: The Passage Inn, Topsham to which Figure 1 refers.

from photographs it is worth making a note of any peculiarities in keystones, cills and modelled ornament. For example the South West is particularly rich in examples of Coade Stone, a moulded artificial stone of Georgian times, and balcony brackets, consoles, and keystones were often made of this material showing moulded heads in deep relief and all forms of elaborate enrichment which added greatly to the impact of the design. A lot of this detail can be readily modelled and, particularly in the larger scales, is essential for a convincing piece of work.

(d) Type of roofing materials used, pitches of roofs, bargeboards if any, projection of eaves, location and type of rainwater pipes and any other external plumbing.

The roof pitch can be difficult to determine, the easiest method being to count the number of brick courses to eaves and ridge and calculate the respective heights in this manner.

However the following roof slopes may be taken as a fairly accurate guide:-

Corrugated iron	min 12°
Slates	min 26°
Pantiles	min 33°
Plain tiles (Staffordshires) thatch and shingles	min 45°

It will be appreciated also that flat roofs are rarely if ever perfectly flat although there was a fashion for this some 20 years ago, the theory being that a permanent covering of water on the roof protected the asphalt. This delusion led to endless trouble and expense and was rapidly discontinued.

A note on the size of various roofing materials will probably be useful:-

Slates (large 'Duchess')	24in × 12in
Slates (small 'Doubles')	12in × 8in
Plain tiles	10½in × 6½in

Cleft shingles vary in size from a width of 4in to 6in to a length of 12in to 27in. (It must be remembered that slates, tiles and shingles provide a double layer and only show half their length or thereabouts).

Pantiles are double curved and are somewhat complicated to model. Their size is 14in × 9in and they are laid to a lap of only 3in showing 11in on the roof slope.

Record sketch of church architecture.

With regard to the remainder of the roof detailing, the ridge tiles should be noted, commonly half round on pantiled roofs, plain angled clay on plain tiles and often also on slated roofs where the ridge gives a welcome touch of colour to contrast with the bluish grey of Welsh slate. Hips are usually finished in half round tiles not forgetting the wrought iron scroll at the foot of the hip to prevent any slip. On high quality tiled roofs 'Granny bonnet' hip tiles are popular, so called for their resemblance to a Victorian sun bonnet.

Rainwater goods are commonly in cast iron and painted to suit the colour scheme of the building:

Rainwater downpipes are usually 3in in diameter although in Georgian town houses they were often square in section and hand made from lead sheet anything up to 6in × 6in. Mediaeval roofs usually discharged their water straight into the street when they were built but in later years are usually found with lead eaves gutters and fall pipes. Rainwater

eaves gutters (half round or ogee) were from 4in to 6in in width and supported on wrought iron brackets at 3ft 0in centres.

Cast iron soil and vent pipes are usually 4in in diameter. All external pipes are usually supplied in 6ft 0in lengths which is worth remembering as it provides a useful check on heights generally. It should be noted that rainwater pipes and so on are held off the wall by small wooden bobbins behind the ears cast on the pipes so you should be able to see daylight behind them on the model!

An interest in modelling will add immeasurably to your enjoyment of holiday trips and outings and while a notebook is valuable for remembering small details, the camera is really the most important aid the modeller can carry. All my record photographs are taken in black and white and enlarged later as necessary on matt paper for the reason stated earlier. Of course the occasional colour shot will be found of value to assist with the finishes of the model.

Record sketch of small town group.

2

Modelling Equipment

While it is usual in a book of this type to give a list of general tools necessary for the practice of the art, modelling architecture covers such a very wide field, can utilise such a variety of materials and media and is dependent to such an extent on the personal techniques and artistic talents of the modeller that to be absolutely specific is somewhat difficult.

The first requirement is of course somewhere to work, and that somewhere must be well and adequately lit. It is quite impossible to do precision work unless you can clearly see what you are doing. Daylight is of course the ideal and therefore your modelling table or bench should face the window so that the shadows of your tools, tee square, etc, are not thrown forward onto the work. If that window faces

north so much the better as then you will not be troubled by strong, direct sunlight on the working surface which is very tiring to the eyes. Solar heat, incidentally, can play havoc with plastic materials. When natural lighting is not possible, and usually the spare time available for modelling is only to be found in the evenings, then a really good artificial light is essential. I have found an Anglepoise lamp to fill this requirement very satisfactorily, and if placed at the top left hand corner of the working surface the counterbalanced arms will allow the positioning of the light wherever required. You will find that the lamp fitted onto a heavy portable base is more satisfactory than the clamp type. It can be moved around with little difficulty and if in more advanced work we indulge in the luxury of

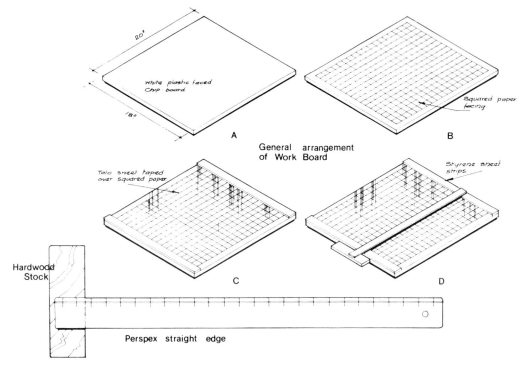

20°

White plastic faced
Chip board.

18°

A

Squared paper
facing

B

General arrangement
of Work Board

Talc sheet taped
over squared paper

Styrene sheet
strips

C

D

Hardwood
Stock

Perspex straight edge

Figure 2.

a miniature lathe, it is better to bring the lamp to the work rather than the reverse. Needless to say when carrying your Anglepoise lift it by the base, never by the arms and never fit a bulb larger than 60 watts; the apparatus is intended as a source of light rather than heat!

Fluorescent lighting is quite unsuitable for the work room; apart from the generally harsh quality of the light, it also has a stroboscopic effect on machine tools and any colour work carried out under its influence will look entirely false when later examined in daylight. Tungsten lighting is, of course, by no means perfect for our purposes as it adversely affects colours, being much warmer than daylight, but any slight colour cast is more readily corrected.

Having satisfactorily organised the lighting, the next prime requirement is the work board. It is perfectly possible and quite adequate to use an ordinary drawing board and tee square for this but it is an expensive solution and therefore not to be recommended. The work board I suggest is shown in figure 2. It is portable, easy to make, and if in a moment of unguarded enthusiasm you use it for heavy cutting with a chisel or craft knife, it will not cost very much to replace.

The work board consists of a sheet of white plastic faced chipboard sold under a variety of trade names and available from any DIY supplier. The overall size is 20in × 18in but as we want to use one of the machine applied edges as a straight edge, ask the supplier to cut it from 2ft wide material, and while you are about it get him to cut two or three as spares. It is often very useful to leave work in progress taped to one board while carrying out detail work on another.

Now cover the working face of the board with squared paper of a scale as near as possible as that to which you work. I use a type with grid lines at 2mm intervals with heavier ruling at 10mm. The squared paper should be taped to the board, square with the working edge, using drafting or masking tape, a supply of which should always be readily to hand. Then over the squared paper place a sheet of talc, taped to the top and bottom of the board when the talc should be bent at right angles to leave a completely unobstructed working surface. Incidentally the squared paper and talc can be obtained from any artist's supplier or drawing office materials merchant at negligible cost.

The last thing we require is a square to enable us to draw truly parallel lines on the work, for which of course a tee square is more than adequate. I have found the square shown in the illustration to serve the purpose very well, again at little cost. It must be remembered that in modelling work there is more than an average risk of boards, squares and similar equipment being damaged inadvertently and therefore the cheaper they are to replace, the less inhibited you will feel in your work.

The tee square I use is made from a 50cm perspex straight edge, the working edge is bevelled and divided into millimetres, the non working edge being undercut which helps to reduce drag on the board surface. The supplier of the perspex straight edge is Cumberland Graphics, trade name 'Rolinx' and obtainable at any branch of W.H. Smith & Son. The stock is fabricated from a 6in length of 2in × 1in hardwood, glued and screwed with countersunk brass screws to the plastic blade. The result, an instrument of considerable refinement and accuracy and it does not even cost a pound – what more could one ask? As you will spend a lot of time at your work board, it pays to take care with its fabrication. Smooth off any rough edges with fine sandpaper, keep it clean by wiping over occasionally with a rag having a trace of methylated spirit on it and never, but never, insert drawing pins into your work surface to hold the work being handled. The heads of the pins will score the underside of your square, the pins themselves will create holes in the working surface which will be found with unerring accuracy by your pencil, every time you draw a line upon it.

A final refinement are the two strips of styrene sheet of variable thickness, dependent upon the thickness of the work being executed, which are attached by means of double sided Sellotape to each side of the work board. These effectively lift the blade of the square clear of the work and avoid the danger of smudged lines when preparing glazing sheets and the risk of scratching the surface of the glazing if a particle of grit is caught by the underside of the tee square. This set up will also be found to be ideal for lining out coach sides, the thickness of the styrene strips being adjusted to hold the blade of the square about 1mm above the work.

To complete our setting out equipment, a good adjustable set square is essential. It is of course possible to set out various angles using a protractor, and 30 and 45 degree fixed angle squares undoubtedly have their uses, but you will be operating under a serious handicap

without an adjustable square. It is one of the facts of life that roof pitches vary enormously and if for example you are setting out a slated roof of a pitch of $28\frac{1}{2}$ degrees, the only way you can be assured of accuracy at the gables is by using a square with a variable blade. The cost of such an instrument can vary between about £3.50 and £15. My advice is to purchase the best you can afford. It will give you a lifetime's service if treated with reasonable care.

The modeller will also require the following drawing instruments which may be purchased as and when required in the programme of work:

1 A set of spring bows, ie, with pencil, pen and divider points. These are required for setting out glazing bars in circular headed windows and fanlights and for drawing segmental arches and the like. The spring bows with divider points, apart from their use in setting out, are indispensable for cutting out arches, circular windows, etc, in styrene sheet. All that is necessary is to set the instruments to the radius required and rotate them on the work with moderate pressure. It will be found that the needle point will score a groove in the sheet and the opening can then be snapped out quite easily.

2 One or two draughtsman's bow pens. Again these are primarily used for drawing in glazing bars, transomes, etc, but they are indispensible in the whole field of modelling wherever it is necessary to draw a line of accurate width and length, particularly lining-out rolling stock, locomotives and coaches, trimming-in string courses, pointing arches – the list is endless.

3 The modeller will also require a selection of pencils, and, in particular, felt tip pens of various colours.

A word or two is also necessary about modern draughting aids, in particular tubular feed pens. They are very popular in the modern drawing office, and are obtainable in a variety of widths and styles. They save an enormous amount of time but unfortunately, generally speaking, they are of little use for our purpose. Only the inks specially prepared for them may be used, otherwise the ink feed will clog with disastrous and usually expensive results.

One side effect of the popularity of the tubular feed pen which the modeller can turn to his advantage is the ready availability of the older traditional drawing instruments on the second hand market. By keeping an eye on antique and second hand shops you can often purchase for a few pounds an old set of drawing instruments, perhaps in electrum, and of excellent quality. The case usually contains three or four bow pens, a set of spring bows and compasses of various types and sizes. Of course you must expect to replace many of the needle points which are often broken or missing but spares may be obtained at most drawing office supplies shops. I may say that some of the instruments I use must be getting on for 80 to 100 years old; they give excellent service and only require regular cleaning to keep them in tip top condition.

We now come to the modelling tools proper. Many will probably already be available in the household tool chest but I append a complete list which can be varied according to your style of modelling and the materials you propose to use.

1. Steel straight edges, at least two of which should be 18in to 2ft 0in in length.
2. An engineer's steel square.
3. A good craft knife. I tend to use the type with break off blades as they encourage you always to use a sharp edge on the work.
4. A small piece of plate glass say 12in square (I use an old piece of mirror). This will be found indispensable. The model is assembled on the glass and you can readily see from the reflection whether any wall, door opening, buttress and so on is out of square. It has the added advantage that the most commonly used adhesives will not readily bond to glass.
5. A small razor saw.
6. A small drill and a selection of drill bits. In addition to the normal size electric drill (bench mounted), I make a great deal of use of a 12 volt miniature drill which is operated through a model transformer. This has the advantage that the speed can be varied to suit the work in hand (If you drill styrene sheet at too high a speed the material will melt and

lock the drill in place, usually resulting in a broken point). A whole range of attachments can be obtained for these small electric drills and in particular they can be used as miniature lathes, which is most useful when fabricating columns, chimney pots and similar fittings.

7. A small mitre block.
8. One or two small chisels which must be kept sharp.
9. One or two small pairs of pliers, flat nosed and round nosed.
10. One or two small wire cutters, both end and side cutting types.
11. Several pairs of tweezers, which should be kept exclusively for your work, otherwise they have an unfortunate habit of disappearing.
12. A pair of very sharp scissors (I use surgical stitch scissors which are carefully hidden away and used only for very fine cutting and trimming).
13. A very fine sandpaper block with replaceable sheets.
14. A small vice is also extremely useful but not absolutely essential for this type of modelling. I have found a 'Mole' Rak Clamp to be as good as a third hand in architectural modelling. It comes fitted with nylon jaws and can be used generally as a replacement for the vice. If however, the Mole clamp is used fitted into the vice, the combination has almost as many possible permutations as an instrument vice but with somewhat greater stability.
15. A piercing saw and a selection of fine blades. You will find that precise cutting in metal or plastic for balustrades, stair strings and similar fittings is readily effected with this tool. In use, let the saw feed itself into the work, use a suitable lubricant (turpentine for metal, water for plastic) and above all do not apply undue pressure on the blade.
16. A fretsaw will also be found very useful on occasions and if you are the possessor of an electric drill, a fretsaw attachment can be purchased which fits on the spindle, in addition to a range of other attachments of varying degrees of usefulness.

17 Finally, as we shall be dealing with plastic modelling materials which include plaster of paris as well as many of the proprietary compounds, we shall require some simple modelling tools including two or three palette knives of which one should be trowel shaped.

3
Modelling Materials

As the quantity of material required in small scale modelling is comparatively small, I have always considered it to be a false economy to make very much use of scrap materials, packing cardboard and the like, although of course there are exceptions. As by far the greatest element in the exercise is likely to be your own time, it seems to be a matter of simple self consideration not to make difficulties for yourself by attempting to work with unsuitable materials.

Depending on the particular technique you adopt, a small stock of raw materials should be built up selected from the following:

1 Cardboard

Card of one sort or another forms a major element in most models. For the carcass of the building, particularly when the external wall finish is to be in brickwork or a smooth stone finish, the best material to use is artist's water colour board with a not pressed or hot pressed face, dependent on the texture you wish to achieve.

For pavements, roadways and general construction I have found ordinary mounting board to be ideal. It can be purchased in a whole range of colours, it takes water and poster colours with no difficulty and perhaps most important of all, it cuts cleanly with a good sharp edge.

For roof tiles and slates and finer modelling to frames and fences, I make much use of ordinary postcards, mainly, I suppose, for general convenience. They may be purchased in packets of 100 and are invaluable for a variety of work.

2 Wood

You will be surprised to find how heavy the average model can become, particularly if much use is made of the thicker grades of styrene sheet and perspex, and because of this, for the general framing and reinforcement of the work I invariably use balsawood. Time was when balsa could be purchased very cheaply indeed and in a range of grades and sizes. Alas those days are no more but nevertheless it will pay to stock up with a dozen or so sheets of balsa in various thicknesses ranging from ⅛in to ½in, in widths from 3in to 6in and length about 36in. If you are serious about your modelling, you will use a considerable amount of balsa and my advice is to buy in bulk, for you will find it to be much more economical than purchasing sheets as the need arises.

For baseboards and larger structures you will require a few sheets of plywood from about 4mm to 8mm in thickness. I use the resin bonded marine type; it costs a little extra but you have the assurance that the laminations will not tend to separate if exposed to damp conditions.

A characteristic of building generally is the amount of timber used in the work and I find that the elusive character and 'feel' of a project is more easily captured if the model reflects the materials of the prototype. Hence my entrance doors are of wood, as are the shutters, the half timbering on a mediaeval jettied front, the hardwood frames of oriel windows – you will find that the slight grain of wood together with its subtle variation in colour gives considerable authenticity to the model. For this small scale detailing I use wood veneer bought in bundles and sold mainly for marquetry. Keep clear of the darker African hardwoods with very open grain. They are of little use for our purpose, but beech, mahogany, sapele, afromosia, and the lighter hardwoods with fine grain look most convincing when finished with a lick of eggshell varnish.

And last but by no means least, a small stock of stripwood will be found most useful, particularly for larger scale models, or when your work includes a whole section of scenery, a complete street, perhaps, or a small village. Timber dowelling also has its uses for the manufacture of columns and the like, although to be truthful, I have found most commercial dowelling to be too coarse for fine work in forming say the capitals and bases; the mouldings simply break away. A much more useful dowelling material can be purchased from most chemists where it is sold as 'orange sticks'. These are dowels of very soft wood which cuts like butter and can be turned to provide columns, chimney pots, urns, in fact a whole variety of accessories with the greatest of ease.

3   Plastic Sheets

It would probably be true to say that the appearance of styrene sheet on the modelling market has revolutionized the whole approach to small scale modelling and immeasurably increased the range of the amateur modeller.

Styrene sheet is obtainable in a range of sheet sizes from approximately 13in × 10in up to 36in × 24in or even greater and is sold under a variety of trade names of which probably 'Plastikard' marketed by Messrs Slaters, of Timperley, Cheshire is best known to the enthusiast. A range of thicknesses is available varying from .010in to .080in or even thicker although the latter is generally as far as the average modeller will require to go, anything more substantial being more easily fabricated from thin plywood.

The considerable advantage of styrene sheeting is an almost complete absence of grain which means that complicated shapes can be cut with great facility and in this respect it can be worked almost like metal as it can be filed and sawn as well as trimmed with a modelling knife. It is a thermoplastic material which means of course that it can be shaped by the application of heat. Curves of any type can be made by taping the sheet to a suitable former and immersing in nearly boiling water, or alternatively placing in a low heat such as that provided by a domestic electric oven. The material cannot be treated like card – whereas card can be scored and bent to form the shape required, styrene sheet cannot. It is brittle, and unless heat is applied it will break if bending is attempted.

The second great advantage afforded by the material is the ease with which it can be joined to form the model by the use of a suitable solvent applied with a brush. Capillary attraction draws the solvent into the joint and the operation is so precise, that work of the utmost refinement and accuracy can be achieved. In addition the joint is usually safe to handle in about a minute or so, allowing the work to proceed in a smooth and unhindered manner.

With all these virtues, are there no disadvantages in the use of the material? Regrettably there are. Styrene sheet is very prone to warping and care must be taken in the general construction to avoid sealing in any enclosed spaces where the solvent cannot readily evaporate. It can result in the most lamentable distortions to a finished model, so proceed with care. Styrene sheet will also not bond readily to other materials and in addition it has a coefficient of thermal expansion somewhat different from that of timber, glass and other commonly used modelling materials.

And a final warning. The liquid solvent used as an adhesive has a moderate degree of toxicity and therefore you should work in a well ventilated space and exercise a reasonable degree of care in the use and storage of the fluid.

Styrene sheet can also be obtained in a wide range of surface textures, including brickwork, random stone, slate, planking, corrugated sheeting and tiles. These have their uses, but personally I am not greatly enamoured of machine applied textures; their very regularity works against them and in the finished model, does much to reduce the artistic quality of the work.

For glazing, a transparent sheet sold as 'Plastiglaze' is available and I would recommend it for small domestic windows, particularly in a styrene sheet model. It is available in two thicknesses, it takes white oil paint very well so that glazing bars and frames can be drawn with little difficulty, and with care it can be scored and bent to form bay windows and lantern lights very neatly indeed. The patent glazing to hipped station canopies can also be very well made of this material.

For bigger windows such as shop displays, and the regular fenestration of large modern buildings, something a little more substantial is required. A characteristic of glazing generally is that it reflects the light and in so doing magnifies any inaccuracies that may have crept into the work. Therefore for this larger scale fabrication there is nothing to better the use of Perspex. This material can be obtained in a variety of thicknesses although for our purposes ⅛in is generally the handiest. It is also manufactured in a dazzling range of colours and textures and in varying types of translucency. When first obtained from the dealer you will find that both sides of the perspex sheet are protected with a layer of brown gummed paper. A word of advice, leave this in position and mark out the work on the paper, not on the exposed transparent sheeting. The easiest way I find of cutting perspex is with a fretsaw and you will find it very easy to follow the drawn line on the protective paper, cutting both the paper and the perspex as one. In addition the underside of the perspex is protected by the gummed paper as it is turned on the cutting table.

It is worth remembering that it is very, very easy to scratch perspex when cutting to shape or in ordinary handling and it is well worth taking care in the initial stages to avoid the laborious chore of polishing out the scratches with metal polish and jeweller's rouge, a most unrewarding activity.

4 Modelling Pastes and Plasters

There are a number of modelling pastes readily available on the market and to be frank I have found very little difference between the various brands. Some are, perhaps, a little smoother in texture and of this group I have found Das, an Italian made paste, to be extremely useful. It will work to quite fine detail, and as it will take impressions well, it can occasionally be used in lieu of plaster for the preparation of moulds and the like.

Pecoscene is another paste of rather coarser texture which is very handy for the representation of roughcast finishes and the more open grained stonework in rubble walling.

Various fire cements and clays are usually stocked by the local ironmonger and these include Kos fire cement and Pyruma fireclay, both very useful and obtainable in somewhat larger sizes than the clays sold specifically for modellers.

In using modelling clays generally, it pays to follow a routine of working which wastes as little material as possible and ensures that your main stock is not exposed to the drying effect of the air. Only take out of the stock tin sufficient clay for the work immediately to hand and at once reseal the tin. To ensure that the stock clay remains at a workable consistency, it is my practice to place a piece of coarse cloth wrung out in water over the clay in the tin before resealing the lid. Using reasonable care, modelling clay can be kept in a workable and satisfactory state for a period of years.

Of course these modelling pastes may be let down with water to a consistency resembling thickish cream and in this condition can be used in a draughtsman's bow pen to indicate 'tuck' jointed stonework, and to add a little extra modelling to such things as keystones or tooled quoins.

Of the plasters available to the modeller, probably the most convenient in use is Polyfilla in its various grades. Providing that an adequate key has been formed, a coating of Polyfilla over a styrene sheet base can give an excellent representation of rendered brickwork, it can be worked to a fine edge and gives particularly neat reveals to windows and doors. I have however found dental plaster to be an excellent general purpose material capable of reproducing the finest detail. It sets very rapidly indeed, in about 20 minutes, but this can be more of an asset than a hindrance. As it hardens it can be carved with the modelling knife with comparative ease so that coursed brickwork, ashlar, and similar finishes provide few problems. Furthermore, detail can be easily worked on detail as it is a simple matter to make a plaster cast of the elevation under construction, carve any relief features on the cast and then recast once more to gain a positive image. If the subject of your model is a very elaborate building with much carved enrichment, elaborate pilasters and so on, then dental plaster is the material to use.

5 Adhesives

Evo-stik Resin 'W' Adhesive. Formulated originally for cabinet makers and joiners, this is one of the most useful glues available to the modeller. It is supplied in plastic containers of various sizes, is available for immediate use and provides a strong, transparent bond for wood, card, building papers, slates and tiles and general framing.
Evo-stik 528 Impact Adhesive. Useful for bond-

ing plastic sheets to wood, also for fibre boards, metal and fabric.

Bostik 1 Clear. A handy general purpose spirit based adhesive, quick drying and clean in working. It is waterproof and sticks, wood, plastic, leather, card and glass.

Apart from the three general purpose adhesives referred to above, there is a considerable range of specialist preparations designed for specific materials

Uhu Clear Adhesive. A quick drying all purpose glue suitable for almost all materials including styrene sheet and in particular Plastiglaze. You will find it especially useful for inserting windows in your models as it will not spread over the surface of the glazing as polystyrene fluid cement will. Its only drawback is a strong tendency to 'string' which can be a nuisance.

Slater's Mek-pak, Britfix Liquid Poly 70 are two popular fluid cements for styrene sheets and styrene generally. They are extremely useful but slightly toxic and should be used in a well ventilated area.

Plastic Weld is a specialist liquid cement designed specifically for acrylic sheet, butyrate and perspex although it will bond styrene sheet with no difficulty. It replaces chloroform which was formerly used in working with perspex but it is by no means a completely safe preparation. The vapour is harmful in unventilated areas both to the eyes and the lungs and contact with the skin should be avoided.

Cyanoacrylate Adhesives have only recently appeared on the market and are sold under a variety of trade names – Super Glue 3, Kung Fu Glue, etc. They will bond in seconds and that means they will stick your fingers together in the same period of time unless handled with care. I very rarely use them as the very rapid bonding usually leaves insufficient time to place the sections being glued accurately and subsequent adjustment is of course quite impossible. They have their uses, usually as an emergency measure when other adhesives have failed. The vapour is however, extremely irritating to the eyes and this drawback taken with the very real possibility of skin bonding, very much reduces their general usefulness. I am somewhat surprised that so far there have been no limiting regulations on the sale of this compound, particularly to children. The risks inherent in its use, particularly in unskilled hands are very real.

Before leaving the subject of adhesives, I must mention the epoxy resins normally supplied in two parts, the adhesive and the hardener which are mixed just before being used.

Araldite Rapid Epoxy will bond metals, glass, rubber, wood, polystyrene very effectively and sets sufficiently hard to allow careful handling in about 10 minutes although it achieves its ultimate hardness in about eight hours.

Devcon 5 Minute Epoxy has similar properties to Araldite but if anything is slightly faster working, hardening in from four to seven minutes but here again ultimate strength is not achieved until eight hours or so.

All epoxy resins are skin irritants and should be handled with reasonable care, washing the hands carefully after use.

6 Adhesive Tapes

Probably the most useful aid available to the modeller is ordinary masking tape. It can be used to attach the elevations to your work board as they are detailed, it has a multiplicity of uses as a temporary hold while other adhesives are setting, it can be used for its original purpose of providing a neat and accurate line between adjacent colours during the finishing process; in short, it is quite invaluable. Buy the largest size reel you can obtain from your local DIY shop.

I also keep on hand a reel of double sided Sellotape as it is so useful for the attachment of last minute details to your work where a fluid adhesive might be a risk to the finish of surrounding modelling. Incidentally this type of tape offers a neat and reliable fixing for engraved name and number plates to the finished paintwork of your model locomotives with the added advantage that they can be removed without damage to the paint should you decide on an alternative identity for your model at some future date.

Finally, a reel of ordinary Sellotape should be on hand for general use, but in particular for the attachment of glazing to window reveals and the like. By the way, if you break through the transparent sheet when forming up a bay window, an invisible repair can be effected with a piece of Sellotape cut to the exact size of the glazing and pressed well down so that no air bubbles are trapped.

7 Building Papers

Although whenever possible I prefer to represent brick, stone, slates, etc, by an appropriate modelling technique to capture the texture and colour, printed papers have their uses, particularly for brickwork which can be very tedious to model by hand. I have found the Superquick building papers to be very convincing, particularly if the rather uniform colouring is toned down with an appropriately graded water colour wash, and if the odd stretcher is picked out in body colour this will give added texture to the work. Before attaching brickpaper to the body of the model, I lay the sheet over a piece of coarse sandpaper and press over the whole area with the heel of the hand. This imparts a granular texture to the brickpaper and greatly improves its realism.

Faller of Gutenbach in the Black Forest produces a most useful series of printed and embossed cards which represent various types of coursed walling stones very convincingly. In particular their sheets of cobblestone or pavé are the best I have come across and are an excellent solution to this somewhat difficult problem.

In addition this enterprising company offers packets of rolled steel sections, roof sections and rainwater fittings which are most useful. Most of their products are readily available in the UK from specialist model shops but if any difficulty is experienced, then a letter to the distributor at 8, Albion Street, Brighton BN2 2NA will solve the problem.

8 Colours

The modeller has a wide choice of colours for finishing his work, all usually excellent quality and readily available. I have found the range offered by Humbrol to be very convenient, reasonably quick drying, of good consistency, and you can mix the shades to any tint you may require. In modelling architecture it is important to use only matt finishes as a hint of gloss to the paint destroys any illusion of reality. The glossy finish of paintwork does not lend itself to scaling down. Even model cars are better finished with an eggshell surface despite the highly polished coachwork of the prototype.

Varnishes should be approached with caution. For some reason I have found even Humbrol matt varnish to be a very erratic performer, a brand new tin, carefully stirred and applied in a warm room drying occasionally with a gloss finish which was quite unacceptable. Be warned therefore. Try out a brushful or

two of the varnish you propose on a surface similar to that of the model and wait for it to dry before committing yourself any further.

In addition to the Humbrol enamels, I keep on hand half a dozen tubes of artist's oil paint to give a little more variety of tint, particularly to slated or tiled roofs where the flexibility of tone afforded by tube colours can be most useful. A tube each of flake white, charcoal grey, yellow ochre, burnt sienna, sap green, and burnt umber are all that are required. To give a little body to the paint where a brushed texture is desirable, you will find that the addition of a little linseed oil medium can be helpful.

A small box of water colours is the final requirement under this heading. They have many uses from tinting in the edges of building papers, to adding the lichen and the general weathering to roofs and stonework. The business of mixing oils with water colours is a very useful hint. If for example you wished to copy the stippled effect of old random stonework, the main body of the wall should be painted in oil colour, which includes most of the proprietary paints, and when this is dry, variegated washes of sap green, yellow ochre and a little burnt sienna water colour are lightly painted over the surface. The result is a delightful broken tone which would be difficult to achieve in any other way. Water colours are useful also for general weathering of locomotives and rolling stock and have the considerable advantage that they can be easily removed with a damp sponge, should you be dissatisfied with the finished effect.

Sundry felt tip pens in various colours will be found useful occasionally as will a black marker pencil for general setting out on styrene sheet, but as these are everyday objects found in the average household there is little point in mentioning them specifically.

A final comment with regard to your brushes. Wash them thoroughly after use and store them in an open jar with their points upwards. If you have been using oil paint, clean them in turpentine or white spirit and when every last trace of colour has been removed, wash them through with soap and water and bring them to a point before storing them away. As the final effect of your models is entirely dependent on the quality of the painting, it pays to take care of your tools. For work of good quality which is of course, what we shall be doing, it is advisable to use only red sable brushes. A selection of sizes from 00 to

5 or 6 will be found more than adequate, supported by a couple of small hog hair brushes for dry brushing and weathering effects. Half a dozen brushes are really all that are required, and given reasonable care in use and storage they will last you for many years.

4
General Construction

A model structure may be made of plaster, card or plastic sheet, or a combination of materials may be used dependent upon the subject and the technique of the modeller. It will probably be found most useful to consider each of these materials in some isolation before relating them to a specific project.

Plaster

Using a totally plastic medium such as a dental plaster, you have no limitation whatsoever in the depth of detail and the complexity of modelling open to you. As a technique however, it can be somewhat messy and requires a little organization to obtain the best results.

The opening procedure is to obtain a sheet of glass and lay it over the elevation on which you are working, figure 3. Then roll out a sheet of plasticine to the depth of your general window and door reveals. Cut from the plasticine the windows and doors trimmed carefully to size and with slightly splayed edges and place in position on the glass sheet over the appropriate doors and windows on the drawing, pressing the plasticine firmly in contact with the glass. Then frame around the elevation with stripwood sealed down to the glass with plasticine.

Before the plaster can be poured, it is necessary to oil the mould to prevent the resultant cast being locked in position. Neatsfoot or olive oil will be found quite suitable, or alternatively a little soft soap is just as good for a few casts.

The plaster is prepared for pouring by gauging with water in a bowl three parts full. Taking a handful of dental plaster and keeping the palm of the hand uppermost, allow the plaster to fall into the water through the fingers until the heap of plaster appears above the surface of the water. Then stir thoroughly but not too fast, the knack being not to trap too many bubbles of air in the mix. Then immediately pour the plaster into the mould, striking the upper surface off to a level finish with a straight edge drawn across the edging stripwood.

Leave the cast for half an hour to harden, then remove the glass sheet from the drawing,

Figure 3.

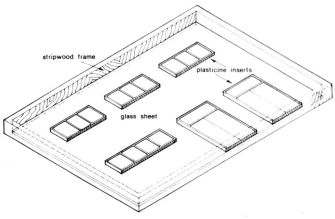

ELEVATIONAL SLAB CASTING

The cottage group shown in Figure 26. Note the main façade cast in plaster.

turn upside down and tap smartly to remove the cast. If a little care is exercised, it is possible to obtain six or seven casts from the one mould. Occasionally the plaster will refuse to come away from the mould, Murphy's Law or more probably suction being the trouble. If the whole sheet is placed under water in the bath or sink, you will find that water will penetrate between the model and the mould and they will then easily separate.

The various plaster slabs forming the walls of the model are easily joined with a little scrim cloth (or open weave bandage) pressed into the joint and immediately covered with liquid plaster.

The plaster elevations can be scribed for brickwork or carved for any type of stone finish very easily indeed, provided the slab is kept fairly damp. In addition, for a quick and very convincing effect, the window recesses can be painted in with waterproof Indian ink and when this has dried, the glazing bars scored into the plaster resulting in a very clean effect with little trouble.

You will find that plaster casting can be somewhat addictive, a type of acquired taste. Once you have mastered the relatively simple

technique involved, you will find yourself using plaster for any number of repetitive elements, retaining walls, buttresses, recessed arches, etc.

One weakness of the plaster model is that it is very susceptible to damage by careless handling, so the finished model should be firmly attached to an adequate sub-base before being located on the layout. Plaster models can however be hardened by immersion in a strong solution of borax which is then gradually heated. After thoroughly drying, the plaster is very hard indeed and can be polished almost like ivory.

Incidentally, dental plaster hardens in 20 minutes or thereabouts so take care to fill your mixing bowls with water before the plaster sets, or better still, do your mixing in pliable plastic bowls and jugs so that in the unhappy event of the plaster actually setting before the utensils have been cleaned, you are not faced with complete disaster.

Of course this technique of plaster casting can be used in association with other materials where the depth of modelling requires it. The small group of shops incorporating Station Road Stores and an antique shop boasts a frontage which, with the exception of the display windows, is almost entirely cast in dental plaster with the detail of the stone courses being

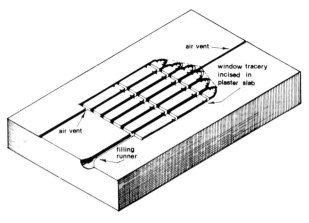

air vent

window tracery
incised in
plaster slab

air vent

filling
runner

PLASTER MOULD CARVING

Figure 4.

cut in later after the plaster slab had been painted so that the effect of recessed cement pointing could be achieved. Incidentally when joining a plaster slab to, for example, styrene sheet, you will find it advisable to give the plaster a thin priming coat of 'Uhu' and allow it to dry before making the final bond.

Before leaving the use of dental plaster in model making, it may be found helpful to touch on the technique of casting from a plaster slab which is useful in the construction of church window tracery, fencing, gates, etc, often troublesome to make in plastic or card.

The method consists of casting a slab of plaster in the normal manner against a sheet of glass and when the plaster is hard, the pattern of the tracery is cut into the face of the slab with a sharp craft knife, taking care to keep the plaster damp while the work proceeds to avoid crumbling, figure 4. When the work of incising the detail is completed, the plaster is thoroughly dried, when any number of casts may be obtained by filling the mould with molten solder, preferably the low melt type, which has a much lower melting point than lead and is considerably more fluid. The molten solder will harden quite quickly and then before removing the cast it will be found advantageous to press the metal down into the mould with a wooden spatula. The reason for this procedure is that the metal shrinks slightly as it solidifies, and pressing the still soft solder firmly into contact with the mould greatly improves the definition of the casting.

It will be appreciated that such casts have little strength but I have found it an ideal way of reproducing the complicated bar tracery so typical of the Decorated and Perpendicular periods of Church architecture. The lack of strength is of no great importance providing the tracery is handled with care, as on the model it is firmly attached to the glazing material which, unlike the prototype, offers considerable support to the completed window.

Cardboard

Card has been a favourite modelling medium for miniature buildings almost since time immemorial. Even Sir Christopher Wren used the material to explore some of his designs in three dimensions. It has many advantages. It is clean in working, it is easy to cut, it takes colour well, it can be curved, it can be bent to sharp angles, it can be built into the most complicated shapes using the simplest of adhesives, it is cheap and above all it is readily available.

Nevertheless with all these inherent advantages, for fine scale modelling I prefer to use styrene sheet. The weakness of cardboard lies in its laminated construction. It is frequently only paper increased in thickness and stiffness by laminating one layer upon another. Thus white cardboard may be sold in thickness described by the number of sheets from very thin 3-sheet to thick 10-sheet.

For general bases I find mounting board to be extremely useful and I include a sketch of the general construction, figure 5. It pays dividends to construct the sub-base of your model early in the programme if for no other reason than the great convenience it affords in handling the

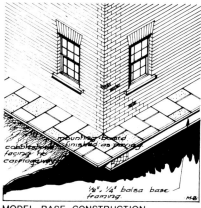

Figure 5. MODEL BASE CONSTRUCTION

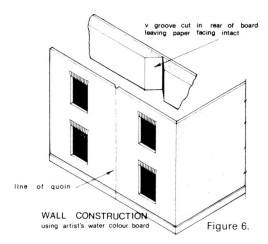

v groove cut in rear of board leaving paper facing intact

line of quoin

WALL CONSTRUCTION
using artist's water colour board   Figure 6.

work. Once the elevations are completed in detail and colour, they should be touched as little as possible and if at an early stage of construction, the body of the model is attached to its base, this will encourage you not to risk soiling finished work. If the model is intended to form part of a village or street scene, it is my practice to use dark grey or brown mounting board for the upper layer of the base and line this out in pencil to simulate paving slabs. As the sketch indicates, the paving oversails the balsa framing, to allow the model to be located conveniently alongside the carriageway.

I cannot emphasise too strongly the desirability of constructing a complicated scenic model in sections, particularly where highly detailed model buildings are concerned. A model invariably requires a certain amount of maintenance over the years — internal lighting may require replacement, due to thermal movement small areas of glazing may become detached, fall pipes may require replacement and so on. You will find it a great help if the model can be lifted clear of the general layout and attended to conveniently and comfortably on your work board. It ensures that any repairs are carried out to the same high standard as the original modelling.

Mounting board forms a useful base for retaining walls, the projecting piers and string courses being very easily fabricated with this material.

For general building construction, particularly for work with a facing brick or stone finish where it is not desired to use a building paper, artist's water colour board has much to commend it.

The elevations are drawn out with care, lined

out for brickwork or stone and finished in water colours before being cut from the sheet. The model is formed up as shown in the drawing, figure 6, by cutting a groove at the back of the sheet where an external angle is required to be formed, care being taken not to cut through the paper facing. The card can then be carefully bent to form the quoin, the coursing of the facing material naturally running through. Detail work such as cills, canopies, keystones and the like are better built up in card and attached to the work with Resin 'W' so that any later touching in can be carried out in water colour to match the general finish.

As with all architectural work, it pays to keep the façades flat for as long as possible and complete all the details you can at this stage, before removing the card from your work board and bending up to form the carcass of the model.

Modelling in card requires careful planning, as any external joints should be so positioned that they are hidden either behind a lean-to addition or attached wing, or in many cases a fall pipe can be located to cover the join exactly. All angles of the building should be reinforced with stripwood and you will find it an advantage to insert some internal walls, not only to reinforce the general structure, but also to avoid the possibility of looking right through the building from front to rear windows.

Porticos, pilasters, pediments and similar embellishments can be made of styrene and attached to a card model with Uhu or other clear spirit based adhesive, but in general attaching plastic to card can be a little troublesome, the bond often proving unreliable. It is preferable not to mix the materials too much.

Plastic Sheets

It is my practice to use the thickest material practicable for the general carcass of the model despite the difficulties this may involve in cutting apertures for windows, doors, and general shaping. The general outline of the elevations can be formed very quickly by scoring to the required line and snapping the material to size. The approach to the fenestration depends very much on the design of the building. If there are a large number of windows of similar size and to a regular pattern you will find it easiest to score vertical lines from ground to eaves on the line of the window reveals and horizontal lines right across the sheet following the levels of the heads and cills. The styrene sheet can then be broken off into sections rather like breaking a toffee bar and then reassembled with the window openings accurately one above the other and true to horizontal level, a matter of some importance if the finish of the building is to be in brick or coursed stone. This approach also avoids the cleaning up which is required particularly to the corners of the apertures if the openings are cut through the sheet in the normal manner.

If the window pattern happens to be irregular and the windows few in number, there is no alternative to cutting the required openings individually through the sheet. As the thinnest styrene I generally use is 0.040in and often 0.060in the easiest way of tackling this matter lies in cutting the openings well inside the marked line using a piercing or fretsaw and finally trimming to size with a sharp craft knife. The work is slightly laborious, but do not be tempted to hurry it as the quality of the model depends very much on the sharpness of the reveals.

As previously mentioned, joining styrene sheet is simplicity itself using one of the recommended fluid adhesives. It is very worthwhile to reinforce the model as the work proceeds, preferably with strips of thick plastic, particularly in the angles and as internal piers for lengthy elevations. Moreover it pays to insert the floors at their appropriate levels. Apart from their use in helping to hold the building square, they prevent the possibility of looking through the upper floor windows all the way through to the ground floor – very destructive of realism! And finally remember to drill a few holes in an inconspicuous position in the floors

and ceilings to allow the fumes from the adhesive to escape. Failure to do so will almost certainly result in warping and twisting of the model.

The assembly of a plastic sheet model should be approached in a methodical manner, completing as much work as possible while the elevations are flat before making any attempt to put them together to form the building. And remember to assemble the work on a sheet of glass, before attaching to the sub-base. The reflected image makes for accuracy and verticality as the eye is deceived so very easily, particularly if you have been working on the detailed sections for a lengthy period of time.

Finally in architectural modelling, it is quite a good guide to follow as far as practicable the method of working or at least the programme of construction of the builders of the prototype. The procedure would therefore be something like the following:

1   Prepare the site, ie, make the sub-base upon which the model is to be located including an indication of any paving, grass and small scale planting, although the addition of larger bushes and trees may with advantage be left until the final stages to assist in bedding the model into the landscape.

2   Prepare all doors and windows and set aside to dry.

3   Construct porches, bay windows, balconies, balustrades, columns and pilasters, etc; complete as individual units and set aside.

4   Cut rainwater pipes, vent pipes and all external plumbing from copper wire of suitable thickness or if you prefer from plastic rod. Form all necessary bends and swan necks, paint and set aside to dry. This will ensure that you do not attempt to paint the back of rainwater pipes when they are attached to the model!

5   Prepare chimney stacks complete with cappings and over-sailing courses, including setting chimney pots in position and flaunching around with modelling paste, cover with brick paper as necessary or otherwise indicate the constructional material and set aside.

6   Cut roof slopes (slightly oversize if you are unsure of the exact dimensions and

anticipate later trimming to fit), cover with squared paper and place under a heavy book or something similar to ensure that no warping takes place as the adhesive dries out.

7 Only now should the external walls of the model be constructed of the chosen material and detailed as much as possible including all windows and doors before leaving the work board.

You will find that a methodical approach such as that suggested will help you to avoid being driven into a corner and compelled to finish a detail by extraordinary means such as with a straight edge placed inside the building while it is propped upside down, or painting the backs of rainwater pipes when they are already in place!

One of the problems which seems to cause the most difficulty for the amateur model maker is the accurate setting out of developed roof planes so that the sloping lines of a pitched roof may be followed convincingly.

The first requirement is an accurate elevation of the roof from both the front and the side, similar to the example show in Figure 7A. I have deliberately chosen a sprocketted roof with a double pitch as they occur very often on the prototype.

A moment's inspection of the elevations reveals that only the dimensions along the

ridge, the eaves, and the break of pitch to the sprocketted section may be taken directly from the drawing; the other dimensions for example BC and AB as they fall away from the eye must be greater than the drawing shows. If however we turn to the side elevation, DE and EF must represent the true height of the roof slopes on the front elevation as they are shown in true elevation on the side.

Therefore to set out the front roof slope, first we draw the line KP which is equal in length to AF on the elevation, and then draw the line LO which is equal in length to BE and set this line at a distance EF from the base, EF being taken from the side elevation. Then the distance DE is measured from line LO and the line MN drawn which is equal to line CD on the elevation, the distance DE being again taken from the side elevation. If we connect the points KLM and NOP we now have the true outline of the roof planes.

If the pitches are consistent all around the roof we can very simply develop the roof planes at the sides from that already drawn for the front elevation. Unfortunately it does not always happen that the builder has been kind enough to simplify the construction in this way. If there is any doubt, it pays to develop the individual roof planes quite independently.

Therefore in Figure 7B for the side elevation, we draw the base line PS which is equal in length to FH on Figure 7A and then insert the break of

Figure 7.

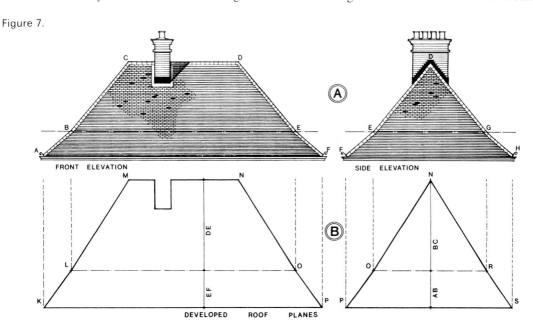

FRONT ELEVATION   SIDE ELEVATION

DEVELOPED   ROOF   PLANES

pitch line OR at the same distance as AB taken from the front elevation, from the base line. The position of the ridge is found by measuring the distance BC again taken from the front elevation. PON and NRS are then joined to form the true outline of the roof plane to the side. You will find that the distances OP and ON on the front and sides are equal. In constructing a sprocketted roof, or for that matter a mansard roof, which has a similar break of pitch, it is necessary to score the sheet to form the shape along the lines LO and OR. Do not overdo the

effect of the sprocketting unless you are making a model of one of the Highland stations which often had a very exaggerated change of pitch as a feature of the design. Apart from their aesthetic appeal, sprockets served a practical purpose in that the easing of the roof slope slowed the speed with which rainwater drained down the roof and helped to ensure that the water was collected in the eaves gutter instead of overshooting and ending down the collars of any unfortunate passers-by.

5
Railway Structures

With the exception of specialised models, practically the first model structure the enthusiast will require is a station; it immediately gives a focal point to the layout, a justification for its existence and a place for trains to arrive and depart. It was while parking my car at the multi-deck park in Exeter that I first noticed the attractive detailing and pleasant proportions of Central Station, a building erected by the Southern Railway in 1933. The first drawing Figure 8 was inspired by this design; it includes a small cupola to lend added interest to the roof and the stone window architraves and classical style entrance portico are in harmony with the neo Georgian flavour of the building.

Before proceeding with the construction of any station it is as well to pay some attention to its location on the layout. The first thing to be borne in mind is that normally the road approach to the building is at platform level which infers that the contours of the layout should be adjusted to achieve this end. There are exceptions, as at Exeter Central where the main station building is at road level over the tracks.

The passenger platforms require fitting at an early stage of the work and they are readily constructed from ½in balsa faced with brick or stone to the supporting walls, the platform

surface being finished with mounting board, ramped down to track level as required. Before finalizing the work to this section, it is essential to ensure that the largest locomotives and longest coaches can pass through the station without fouling the oversailing nosing of the platform edges, particularly if they are sited on a curve. Some model locomotives have over-scale cylinders or valve gear and need larger than scale clearance for platforms.

The location of the station building can now be plotted on the platform, making due allowance for any glazed canopies which may be desirable for the protection of your model passengers, and which will butt up against the brickwork of the main building.

A brief perusal of the drawing will show the essentially very simple nature of the design, the roof which seems to cause the beginner the most difficulty, being set down behind a parapet wall which will most effectively hide any slight inaccuracies in setting out. The hip tiles likewise cover the mitring of the hips and connection with the ridge and it is comparatively easy to make a very tidy job of the slating as the roof can be constructed as an entirely separate structure and simply placed on the base like a lid when all the finishes have been completed.

I constructed this model of styrene sheet and

The Georgian style station shown in Figure 8.

Figure 8.

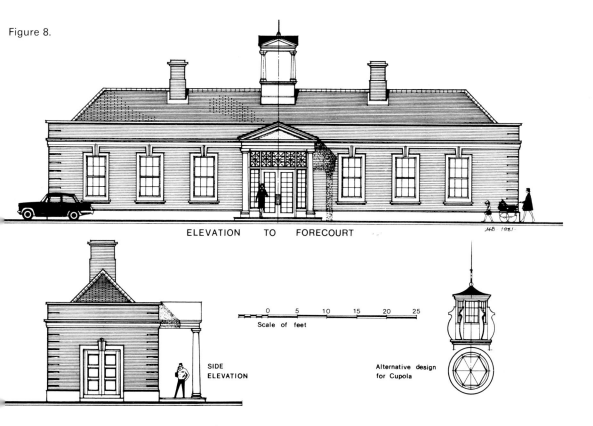

ELEVATION TO FORECOURT

MB 1951

SIDE
ELEVATION

0   5   10   15   20   25
Scale of feet

Alternative design
for Cupola

a start was made by tracing the glazing bars of the windows onto 0.010in 'Plastiglaze' sheet using matt white oil paint in a draughtsman's bow pen. Incidentally the ornamental grill above the transome to the main entrance doors is indicated by drawing the pattern in black indian ink directly on the glazing and very effective it looks too, particularly with the lighting behind it.

The external walls were cut from 0.040in styrene sheet faced with brickpaper, in this case Superquick D1 red brick although this is very much a matter of your personal taste. The stone architraves, base and string courses show well against this finish as a background.

A sheet of 0.060in material was located as a false flat roof at the level of the upper string course and this was painted matt black before the finished slated, hipped roof was set down upon it, the black margin around the perimeter giving a neat imitation of a parapet gutter. Incidentally the parapet wall above gutter level is thickened out with an additional layer of 0.040in material and faced with brickpaper since the inner face can be easily seen from above, this work being carried out before the coping (of 0.040in material) is fixed in position.

It is as well to remember that the roof is usually the first part of the model to be seen by the casual spectator and it therefore behoves us to ensure that this is as visually attractive and well finished as possible. Generally speaking the more complicated and interesting the shape is, the better it will appear and that serves to explain the fitting of the cupola in the present design. Again this ornamental feature is constructed of 0.060in styrene sheet, any necessary curves being formed with the aid of a piercing saw.

The portico was the final part of the work to be tackled and was built of rather thinner material than the main structure. It is important to note the way the moulds mitre into the string course, these being echoed in the raking mouldings within the tympanum of the pediment which looks well if finished in a slightly contrasting colour. The two columns were made from plastic sprue turned slowly in an electric drill, slowly because the files and sandpaper used to form the head and base and the entasis of the shaft generate heat by friction and if you are not careful, the plastic will soften and gently droop into a most depressing curve. All the stone

facings were carefully painted in a flat off white with a flick of yellow ochre in imitation of Beer stone as my layout is set in the West Country, although to be strictly accurate as this is supposed to be a 'Southern' design, the embellishments would be of artificial stone, cast not carved to the architect's taste.

The slates were separately applied to the roof following the lines of the graph paper previously applied to the roof slopes and bedded in place in a coating of Resin W adhesive. Unfortunately there is no short cut to this section of the work. As the slates overlap each other, they form a roof texture which is quite distinctive; ready printed slate paper is a very poor substitute and ruins the quality of the finish in one fell swoop. After you have made one or two models you will quite enjoy the model tiler's trade. The slates or tiles are cut in batches from stacked postcards, picked up by stabbing them with the tip of your modelling knife and then carefully applied to the previously glued surface of the roof slope. The tackiness of the adhesive removes the slate from your knife and you repeat the operation course by course. If it is any consolation, the roof of this model was finished as Delabole slate, which are rather larger than the Welsh variety and this reduces the work involved. Of course the fun comes later in painting the slates which I tend to do with a strange mixture of left over oddments of matt paint mixed with plenty of white since Cornish slate weathers to a very attractive silvery grey. And in the finishing touches do not forget the orange coloured lichen and the visiting cards of the local seagulls spread tastefully along the ridge. These are better indicated with touches of water colour as this gives a most attractive mottled effect, very true to life.

Incidentally the unglazed external doors are formed of wood veneer, in this case slips of sapele, with raised panels (an additional layer of veneer) and finished with a lick of eggshell varnish. The only other detail warranting mention is probably the finish to the brick quoins. These are accented by recessing one course of brickwork in every four courses. It looks effective and is typical of the style.

The photographs on pages 33 and 44 show the platform side of the station building with the extensive protective canopy formed of patent glazing to the hipped roofs. The valleys are set at the level of the string course above the

The platform side of the Georgian station. A Dean 0–6–0 pulls out.

windows of the main structure to ensure that no difficulties arise in setting the glazed canopy to the brickwork.

On the prototype station considerable use was made of roof lights and patent glazing to the passenger platforms and as it is such a typical feature, it gives a very authentic touch to the model.

Pitched glazed roofs are not difficult to model and there is the added bonus that once the roof planes are complete, there is no slating to be done to finish the work.

The construction is commenced by setting out the roofs on 0.020in Plastiglaze following the principles outlined in Chapter 4. The glazing bars are drawn in pale grey matt paint at 2ft scale centres following the pitch of the roof and if you are modelling the underside of the canopy in detail, the bars should be supported by purlins at 8ft centres. Some delightful chemical etched trusses, brackets, and beams, together with cast corbels and columns, are available from the Scale Link Co, which make the completion of this work to a high level of finish, a very pleasurable exercise. Unfortunately when I made my model, these accessories were not available and I fabricated much of the

supporting steelwork from the plastic sections available from Faller, the supporting columns being small bore copper tube and the bases being detailed with a roll formed of parcel tape. The ridges and hips of the patent glazing were finished with a modelled lead roll utilising Slater's Microstrip and rod and painted pale grey to match the glazing bars.

The finishing touch to the canopy is provided by the valance to the platform face with its saw tooth edging and pattern of perforations, each of the individual railway companies having its own distinctive design. Although aesthetically the valance may be of doubtful worth, nevertheless they were a very typical feature of older stations and should be reproduced. It is of course perfectly practicable to fabricate the valance by hand, but the work tends to be rather tedious and it is somewhat difficult to maintain absolute regularity in the divisions of the vertical boarding and the saw tooth edging. As there are several patterns available in varying scales from the trade, both in etched brass and plastic, I strongly advise that advantage should be taken of these offerings.

The design offered in Figure 9 was inspired by a query from a gentleman in Hanover, West Germany who asked why the British railway modeller clung so assiduously to Victorian designs; he was seeking something more up to date to be in harmony with his Inter-City 125 recently purchased on a holiday trip.

The model is basically a perspex box framed up of bronze coloured sheet, the ground and upper floors being constructed as separate units and finally connected by the recessed ring beam at the head of the ground floor windows.

The work is started as usual by tracing the window pattern in silver paint (to reproduce silver anodized aluminium window frames) directly on the perspex. Metallic paints do not dry as rapidly as matt white oils, so set the work aside overnight to ensure that there is no risk of smudging the lining.

The piers between the windows at first floor are modelled as precast concrete panels with an exposed aggregate finish which is most easily

and convincingly represented by coarse sand-paper backed with 0.060in styrene sheet. Do not attempt to carry the sandpaper into the window reveals. These should be painted in matt pale buff, much lighter than the colour of the sandpaper facing. The window pattern is completed by the chair rail cut from pre-painted styrene, the panel below the rail being finished in a dark sepia brown (Humbrol 98) and a lick of eggshell varnish when dry.

The exposed concrete framing, the entrance canopy and columns to the ground floor are cut from obechi sheet, a rather harder wood than balsa but with a very fine grain, sanded to as smooth a finish as possible with clean and sharp arrises (corners), and finally painted with the pale buff used for the window reveals. The ground floor window boxes are simply cut from

Figure 9.

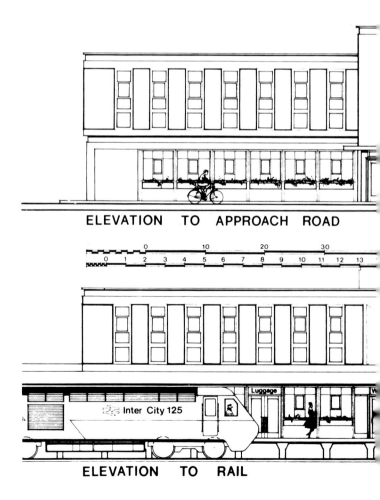

ELEVATION   TO   APPROACH   ROAD

ELEVATION   TO   RAIL

stripwood and filled with vegetation to suit your taste — most conveniently sprigs of 'Woodland Scenics' spring green foliage material, the flowers being indicated by blobs of process white poster colour which when dry are given a dab of fluorescent red, yellow or orange. You will be pleasantly surprised how convincing the effect can be.

The overtrack bridge shown in Figure 10 echoes the architectural style of the main building and is constructed in a similar manner – bronze perspex sides with silver anodised framing. Notice the rather deep fascia which allows for the grain of wheat bulbs used for internal lighting to be set close to the underside of the flat roof. I think that realism suffers badly if the light source is visible in model work. The internal lighting of the main station building will also repay a little thought. The distance between ground and first floor windows and above the first floor window heads is sufficiently great to permit the inclusion of a double floor, or to be more accurate a floor with suspended ceiling. I have had some success using frosted perspex as a ceiling diaphragm and designing a lighting pattern by painting the underside with matt white oil paint, leaving appropriate spaces where a lighting fitting would be installed in the prototype. Grain of wheat bulbs are then fitted above the ceiling and covered by the floor above to which they are fixed with a loop of sellotape. Using this method it is relatively easy to have a prototypical lighting pattern which brings the model to life in a remarkable manner for evening effects. Of course it is essential that the model lighting bulbs should be under-run,

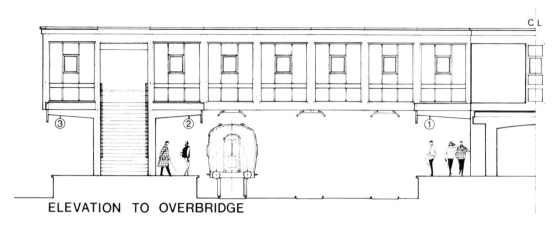

ELEVATION TO OVERBRIDGE

Figure 10.

mainly to prolong their life which can be indefinite if they are supplied with between 6 and 9 volts, when their nominal rating is 12 volts. It is usually a bothersome business replacing lighting units although this possibility must always be faced, and to that end a little forethought in construction should ensure that either the roof or the floor of your model is removable to permit access to the interior for occasional maintenance of this nature.

Island platform structure shown in Figure 12.

Figure 11 sets out details of the access stairways to the overbridge from the secondary platform and requires careful study before setting out the work. The overplatform canopy is pierced by the stair and to preserve an acceptable headroom above the treads, a small monitor roof or upstand bulkhead requires to be formed as is shown in detail in the section. The canopy is assumed to be of reinforced concrete with a double cantilever from the supporting columns and the whole of the structural work should be painted a matt pale

The detail of the bookstall. A Pannier tank shunts in yard.

grey. The upper surfaces of canopies and flat roofs are usually finished with either felt or asphalt and to reproduce this in model form I use dark grey emery paper. The texture and colour are just about right for the purpose and if you fancy some super detailing, assume the roof is felted and score in the jointing lines at about 3ft intervals. This effect can be further improved by drawing a fine line of glossy black enamel where the joints occur; it simulates exactly the appearance of the mastic which is used to fix the felt to the concrete flat and which usually bleeds slightly out of the joint when

exposed to the heat of the sun. As a final detail do not forget the upstand skirting which is applied to the inner side of the parapet wall. It is of course an extension of the asphalt or felt roofing finish and ensures that any water pooling on the flat roof does not penetrate into the surrounding structure.

Flat roofs by their very nature lack the visual interest of the pitched variety with their tiles or slates, dormers and rooflights and some care should be taken in modelling such features reproducing as much of the usually meagre detail as possible.

Stairways seem to cause problems and in

Figure 11.

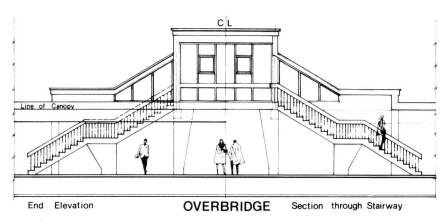

Line of Canopy

C L

End   Elevation   **OVERBRIDGE**   Section   through   Stairway

Close up of covered seating under the island canopy.

browsing through the model railway magazines, I have found one of the greatest give-aways to be the treatment of overbridges and their stairways in particular. The various bye-laws governing public safety require that:

1   Stairways should never have more than 15 risers in any flight. Reflect on the number of model overbridges one sees with the stairway rising from the platform in one continuous flight, often with between 20 or 25 steps. Shame on the modeller for lack of research; the Inspecting Officer of Railways would close his enterprise down with no hesitation!

2   Handrails should not be less than 2ft 9in high measured from the nosing of the step, and on landings this should be increased to at least 3ft 0in and preferably 3ft 6in.

3   the maximum pitch of public stairways is 38 degrees but on stairs with peak traffic conditions, and that applies particularly to your model station, the pitch should be considerably less. Under these circumstances the tread should be 12in and the rise 6.4in giving a very easy going.

Landings should be at least as wide as the stairs and changes in the height of the steps on the same stairway are not permitted, so set you flights out with care before picking up the modelling knife and attacking the styrene.

Staircases can make or mar your model; take your time and check your dimensions as you go along. In construction, first carefully cut out the strings using a piercing saw and cutting the two strings as one by tacking them together before commencing operations. The handrails can be shaped at the same time. Then cut a strip o plastic the exact width of the stair between the strings and the sides precisely parallel. From this the treads and risers can be cut, although the latter are usually dispensed with on over track bridges. Mark the position of the treads on the inside face of the strings and away you go tacking the steps in position with Mekpak to the first string. Check that all the treads are parallel and true and then before the adhesive ha hardened, offer up the opposite string to the free ends of the treads and tack again in place Place the completed stair on your sheet of glas and examine the flight carefully from all angle before making any necessary adjustments with a pair of tweezers and handling very lightl indeed. Then set aside overnight to harde

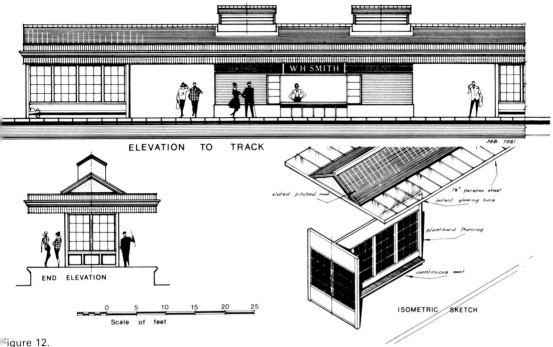

ELEVATION TO TRACK

END ELEVATION

0 5 10 15 20 25
Scale of feet

slated pitched roof

⅛" perspex sheet

patent glazing bars

plastikard framing

continuous seat

ISOMETRIC SKETCH

MB 1981

Figure 12.

thoroughly before commencing work on the handrails. On the overbridge shown in Figure 1 the handrail is supposedly supported on wrought iron balusters which would be leaded into the concrete string at the base and welded to a wrought iron strap at the head which in turn would be screwed to the underside of the hardwood handrail. We model the balustrade by cutting the overall shape from transparent sheet (0.020in Plastiglaze) and drawing the balusters thereon in matt white paint. The handrail proper is then painted a medium brown in imitation of teak (do not attempt to cut the handrails from wood veneer, it splits too easily) and attached to the upper side of your balustrade which is finally cemented to the string of the stair. The finished effect is very convincing and the fact that the balusters are drawn on transparent sheet is not at all evident. This is also an excellent method of reproducing the rather ornate balustrades so beloved by the Georgian and Regency builder. In a later chapter a typical Georgian terrace is detailed and the photograph on page 69 shows quite clearly the manner in which the first floor balconies have been modelled utilizing transparent sheet for the balustrades.

The design offered in Figure 12 is based on an example emanating originally from the Swin-

don drawing office of the former Great Western Railway and used widely over the whole GWR network, especially in the outer London suburbs. The proportions and general detailing are to my mind particularly attractive and the photographs of the finished model show its suitability for a secondary passenger platform which requires additional toilet facilities.

The construction is simplicity itself. The work is commenced by cutting the canopy from ⅛in clear perspex sheet, remembering not to remove the protective gummed paper until the edges have been sanded smooth.

The first operation is to draw on the lines of the patent glazing bars in pale grey oil colour (Humbrol 87 let down with a little flat white). The bars are set at 2ft 6in centres and for the super detailer, are of inverted T section, the lead covering oxidising to a very light grey. When the work is dry, the perimeter valance is added, being attached to the perspex with 'Plastic weld', a liquid adhesive prepared especially for use with perspex. Take care with the moulding attached to the face of the valance and formed from microstrip. The effect will be spoiled unless the line is kept perfectly straight. This can easily be achieved by attaching the moulding with a dab of Mekpak at one end, waiting for the adhesive to attain a hold and

The re-vamped Triang dmu leaves Porthcurno station island platform.

then pulling gently on the other end while running a brushful of adhesive along the mould. If despite everything a kink or two develops in the line, all is not lost. Apply a steel straight edge to the lower edge of the mould and gently press it into contact with the back of your modelling knife until the line is true.

The central structure incorporating a bookstall with toilets at either end is finished in facing brickwork to match the main building. As W.H. Smith & Sons Ltd usually incorporates a glazed panel at each end of the stallriser to house the smaller items of merchandise (pen sets, hard back books, special editions and so forth), they have been included in the model. The fascia lettering was culled from one of the Sunday colour supplements and the general advertisements came from various sources, mainly the miniature sheets marketed by W. & H. Models Ltd., and Pendon Museum. The display counter was decorated with rows of magazines and periodicals cut from coloured paper with flicks of poster paint to indicate the covers, no attempt being made at fine detail, a general effect being all that is required.

The glazed draught screens with their en-closed seating were fabricated from perspex in a similar manner to the canopy and the glazing bars drawn in matt white paint, on both sides of the perspex. If the work is carried out carefully you will get the illusion that the bar penetrates the 'glass'; the close up on page 38 brings this out rather well.

The only remaining section requiring our attention is the pitched, slated roof complete with louvred ventilators above the toilet positions. This is formed of 0.040in styrene sheet squared paper being attached to the upper roof slopes and finished with slates in the usual manner. Pay due respect to the finish at the gable ends which in the prototype offers quite a refined detail, the inset mouldings giving an appearance almost like a classical pediment.

If you require internal lighting to the model the grain of wheat bulbs are conveniently sited within the slated roof structure, one over each of the seat positions and another slightly brighter illuminating the bookstall. I connected the outer bulbs in series to the 9 volt supply but fed direct to the bookstall bulb which received the full voltage. The small amount of extra work is worthwhile if you are fond of night effects.

When the whole of this work was complete, attached the slated roof section to the perspe

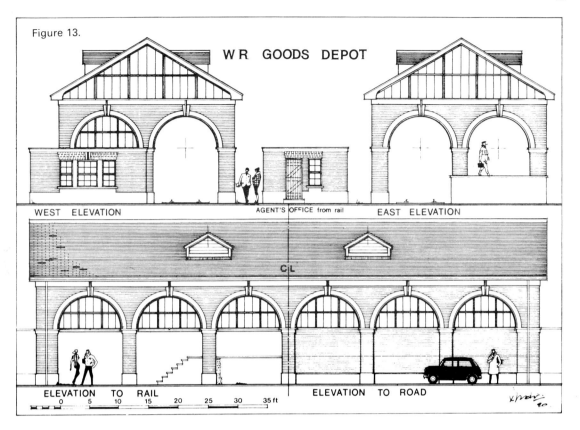

Figure 13.

WR GOODS DEPOT

WEST ELEVATION   AGENT'S OFFICE from rail   EAST ELEVATION

ELEVATION TO RAIL   ELEVATION TO ROAD

0 5 10 15 20 25 30 35 ft

of the canopy with small brass screws let into hardwood blocks previously glued inside the 'loft' space, so to speak. This ensured that access was readily available to this area should one or two of the light bulbs require replacement; Murphy's Law dictates that this will surely happen just as the finished model is proudly located in position for the first time, and the current switched on.

The draught screen/seating units and the central bookstall are firmly attached to the platform surface but I glued the canopy to the upper edges of these units with rubber cement, a joint that is easily broken for any necessary servicing of the canopy and roof.

In the early days of the railways, the station master was a pillar of the local community, ranking as a peer of the parson and the squire, his importance being reflected in the quality of the station house provided for him by the company. The photograph on page 43 shows Topsham station building and is typical of the style adopted by the LSWR in the Gothic revival manner. The stationmaster's accommodation dominates the composition but the single storey booking office wing is detailed to the same relatively high standard. Notice in particular the four-centred arch to the platform entrance door and the bay window with stone mullions to the main waiting room, a window which seems to have caused the designer more than a little difficulty judging by the gymnastics of the leaded roof to the bay and the rainwater gutter behind.

The chimneys are important and never more so than in a model where they add much to the character of the work. Here the treatment of the chimney caps is typical of the period, the oversailing courses proceeding in steps of 2¼in. What is rather less common is the secondary moulding in specially shaped bricks just above the junction of the stack with the roof slope. The present day building is rather spoiled by the coat of Snowcem which has been applied to much of the faced brickwork reducing the contrast of the stone frames and mullions, and the less said about the lighting standards the better!

The goods shed illustrated in Figure 3 is based on a prototype observed from the Penzance

Sketch from south west

Figure 14.

train in the days just after the second world war. The glazed gable ends are typical Western details often encountered in Devon and Cornwall and in my opinion, lend a great deal of interest to the composition. Some peculiar offerings came from the old Swindon drawing office but this design must rank as one of its more inspired efforts.

This is not an easy model to construct and the drawing must be followed absolutely if success is to be assured. At the start of the operation four sheets of Plastikard are tacked together with Mekpak and the arcaded elevations cut out as one using a fretsaw or piercing saw with a fine blade. Take it easy and lubricate the saw with a little water applied with a brush as the work proceeds. Any undue haste and the friction generated by the saw will soften the plastic and lock the blade solidly in the work. The result will be a series of broken blades and probably a heightened blood pressure, which is not the purpose of the exercise.

A feature of the design is the glazed panel filling the tympanum of each arch above the tie bar and in the model this glazing is inserted as a continuous strip between the inner and outer layers of Plastikard, a sandwich construction, leaving the core of the columns to be filled with 0.020in styrene to match the thickness of the glazing material.

The roof above wallplate level is formed as a complete unit attached to the main structure by small brass screws setting into hardwood blocks rather in the manner of the station building already discussed. The internal soffit carries grain of wheat bulbs, under run as usual, to provide that authentic gaslit atmosphere and prolong their life.

Due to the open nature of the design, the interior is very visible and requires to be finished to the same standard as the external elevations. To give a little added visual interest I used a red brick (Superquick D1) for the outer leaf and a yellow brick (Superquick D2) for the interior. Similarly the small flat roofed agent's office to the west of the main building was finished in yellow brick to indicate that this was obviously a later addition to the depot.

The platform was the final part of the model to be constructed and was formed, as is my wont, from mounting board for the upper surface which could be well finished as paving stones and ½in balsa for the supporting walls finished as brickwork to match the remainder of the scheme. Note the internal flight of steps and the increased height of the platform compared with those for passenger use; in many instances the height was adjusted to enable bulk freight such as potatoes, turnips, sawn timber etc to be tipped or shovelled direct into open wagons.

Panoramic view of Porthcurno station with island
platform. The goods shed is in background.

Topsham station. Note the treatment of the bay
window.

The stone facings to the arches are cut with spring bow dividers as explained in Chapter 2, from 0.020in material, the simple column caps, keystones and other details being made up with Slater's microstrip. To ensure that all the capitals are level a length of microstrip was tacked to the face of the arcading running from one end of the building to the other and the capitals formed up using this as a base.

Finally the roof was finished as Delabole slate, care being taken to mitre the courses neatly around the dormer vents which are hardly justified in a building of this open nature, but they do give added interest to what would otherwise be. a rather featureless stretch of slating.

When the goods shed is finally located on your layout, do not omit the clutter which usually surrounded such buildings, boxes and crates (easily fabricated from stripwood) on the platform, or a bicycle or two leaning against the piers. Finally in a depot of this size a hand operated crane would invariably be provided, platform mounted in a convenient position to serve both lorries parked on the access roadway and goods wagons on the adjacent siding.

The main problem involved in the construction of model signal boxes lies in the large area of relatively unsupported glazing, which if constructed from Plastiglaze or other plastic material, talc or celluloid, can lead to difficulties not only due to differential thermal expansion, but also to the nasty habit of plastic glazing in bowing inwards over a period of time throwing off the carefully applied microstrip framing and bringing disaster to the whole structure.

It was for these reasons, that early in my modelling career, I resolved to construct all future signalboxes using glass for the glazing, and for a change the glass could be a support to the main structure instead of the other way around. Casting about for an acceptable source of supply, I first used microscope slides which were satisfactory for GWR designs where the window area is not usually very deep, but not a lot of help for the greenhouse style favoured by the LSWR, or the designs of the Railway Signal Company. I then came upon the thin picture framing glass much used by Victorian craftsmen and a visit to a local auction provided sufficient material for all my future needs, and for a very trifling sum. The only problem lay in accurately cutting the glass to size. At first I used a normal glass cutter fitted with hardened steel wheels but I have to confess that this was far from being a successful operation since I wasted more

The goods shed showing its setting in Porthcurno station yard.

material than I used. What I really needed was a diamond for precision work but the cost of the professional instrument seemed exhorbitant bearing in mind the limited number of signal-boxes required on the average layout. It was while replacing the stylus on my record player that inspiration dawned – the stylus had a diamond head! It was very carefully removed with tweezers and attached with cyanoacrylate adhesive to a short metal rod which could be used in the manner of a pencil. The result, a precision instrument which very much simplified the work. The glass is simply laid over the working drawing, held in place with drafting tape and the panel sizes traced over with the cutter. It is then simplicity itself to snap off the panels over a straight edge. The normal work board can be used for this operation but if you do, remember to lay a square of felt or other thickish fabric over the board before placing the glass on it for cutting. It collects the inevitable fine slivers of glass removed in the operation and at the same time offers a resilient bedding for the glass which absorbs the pressure applied when scribing the material and very much reduces the possibility of unwanted cracking.

One final point, do not attempt to form the window frames and mullions of plastic micro-strip if you are using glass as your base material. I know it is the most convenient solution and initially the plastic adheres perfectly to the glass with a dab of Mekpak. But, and it is a big but, a change in the temperature of the railway room and the plastic will part company with the glass in no uncertain manner, the demon dte (differential thermal expansion) being the culprit. So be warned, I have explored this particular cul-de-sac very thoroughly and bear the scars to prove it!

Figure 15 is based on the standard GWR panel size for its timber framed signalboxes, the peculiar five light sashes dictating the module. The inspiration for this particular drawing came from one of the boxes at Exeter St David's, but has been modified by the addition of an external staircase and storm porch, and the windows to the brick built ground floor are somewhat at variance with the prototype, primarily to reduce the height of the model. The construction provides few problems, the brick ground floor, the weatherboarded first floor and the slated roof being constructed as separate sections and completed in their entirety before finally being brought together to form the complete model. The ground and first floors were cemented together but the roof can be removed to allow

Figure 15.

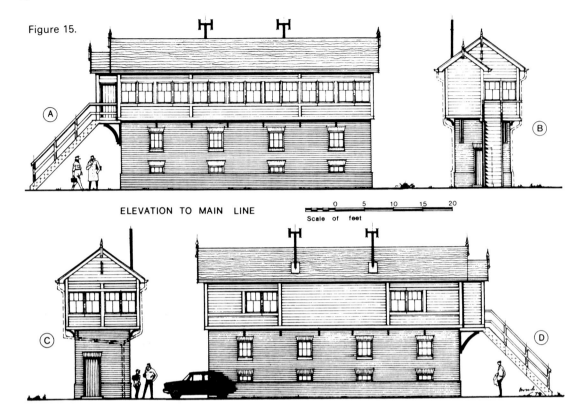

ELEVATION TO MAIN LINE

0 5 10 15 20
Scale of feet

access to the fully fitted interior and the grain of wheat bulb, here supplied with the very minimum of current (have you noticed how dimly lit signalboxes are in real life – carrots must figure prominently on the average signalman's diet!)

To lend additional authenticity to the model, the smaller external details should be modelled with reasonable care. The finials for example are a significant company trade mark filed up from brass scrap and fixed in position with cyanoacrylate for a satisfactory join to the plastic barge boards.

The galvanized steel flue pipes are most easily formed from the small bore copper tubing commonly used for point control and the like, care being required in forming the H type terminal. The flue pipes when completed should be fixed by forcing them into a hole drilled in a small hardwood block mounted on the underside of the roof plane.

Roof details are by their nature prone to accidental damage from arms reaching over the model to attend to the operation of the trains and for this reason should be well and adequately fixed in position. Chimneys should always be taken well down into the body of the model and either glued to a triangular plastic roof truss or pinned securely at the base to a floor. And while we are discussing accidents, remember as an elementary safety precaution to blunt the points of finials fixed to signals and boxes. The method of making such details from needles and small beads, while reproducing the character of the prototype very well, should not be entertained. The upturned steel points are almost guaranteed to cause trouble sooner or later; better a damaged model than a torn hand or even worse. Indeed, on reflection, it would be prudent to manufacture all finials from plastic rod and keep a box of spares handy for ready replacement as necessary.

I think that the designs of the Railway Signal Company Ltd, much used in the North West in the closing years of the nineteenth century, were very attractive. Careful thought has been given to the fenestration, the transom above the main cill allowing the horizontal sliding sashes to be contained within the upper two thirds of the window, the sub lights being glazed directly into the transome and frame.

Figures 16 and 17, while not being based on a specific prototype, nevertheless incorporate the

Detail of the canopy, Georgian station.

The signalbox shown in Figures 16 and 17.

Detail showing the cantilevered toilet and waste pipe.

The rear elevation of the signalbox.

characteristic details developed by this private company which make up into an attractive and typical model.

Construction is quite straightforward and should cause little difficulty. The ship lap weatherboarding to the first floor is mounted on a squared paper backing to ensure the regularity of the work, the boards butting into the corner posts which neatly conceal the thickness of the glazing material, used for the windows. The small square windows in the centres of the gables were introduced for ventilation purposes and were centre pivot hung. If modelled in a half open position they would lend an unusual touch to the signal box; odd details like this give the layout character and individuality.

The grab rails to the first floor windows were

Figure 16.

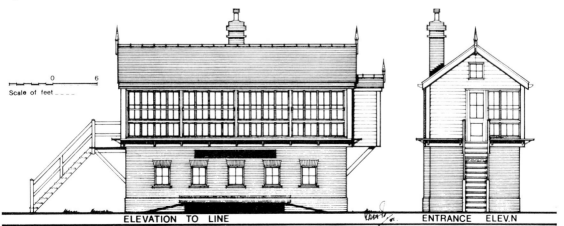

ELEVATION TO LINE   ENTRANCE ELEV.N

Scale of feet

0   6

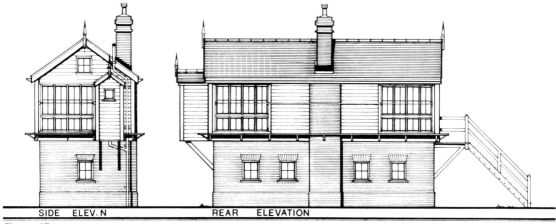

SIDE ELEV. N | REAR ELEVATION

Figure 17.

for the use of the window cleaner and were mounted on ferrules screwed to the frame and mullions. They are easily made from 'stretched sprue' a method borrowed from aircraft modelling. It is as well to select a suitably coloured scrap of plastic, either black or silver, as any attempt to paint the handrail when fixed in place, can easily result in marking the glazing and a slip of this nature is difficult if not impossible to rectify. In addition you will be surprised how a coat of paint increases the thickness of these small details and detracts from the refinement of the work.

The photographs on page 48 show the model mounted on its sub-base before final location on the layout. As mentioned previously, this is my invariable practice as it avoids an unnatural black line at the base of the building and furthermore provides a most convenient handle for detailing the model and applying the final colouring.

Signal boxes designed and in some cases built by the Railway Signal Company Ltd, were by no means confined exclusively to the North; some

examples can be found in South Wales and even west of Bristol so that such a signalbox on God's Wonderful Railway would not be a complete anachronism. As you will see, my model bears the somewhat unlikely location plate of 'Geevor Junction' which by inference places it in the far west of Cornwall where the tin mine of that name is located. I have though been guilty of much worse offences as you will find out rather later in this book – a Hertfordshire malt house in Cornwall and in brickwork of all materials. The planners of Truro would never recover.

The photograph on page 52 is of the signal box at Topsham built by the LSWR. The South Western had a rather cosy style for these structures, quite often a sort of cross between a greenhouse and a woodshed rather well exemplified in this shot. The tiny gabled vent in the slated roof could have been drawn by Walt Disney! I like the way the signalman has painted over the lower panes of the window to give himself a little privacy no doubt from the adjoining roadway – 'Always drinking tea, Henry, no wonder the railway don't pay a

Figure 18.

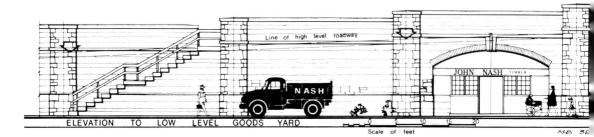

ELEVATION TO LOW LEVEL GOODS YARD

Scale of feet

dividend'. Pity about that lifting barrier in the background and the spot lamps screwed to the fascia; that is called progress.

Retaining walls, particularly in undulating country, form such an important part of the railway scene. Vast stretches of faced brickwork, without a structural break and decorated only by occasional posters appear only too often on the average model layout. The prototype just is not built that way.

Figure 18 attempts to incorporate a variety of treatments to give visual interest to a background retainer, in this case supporting an inclined roadway leading to the station yard. The line of the high level road is indicated by the chain dotted line and it will be noticed that the retaining wall is designed in a series of steps to keep pace with the gradient. This enables the brickwork or stone of which the wall is constructed to be built in level courses (it is most unusual to have the bed joints laid on the rake).

The retaining wall requires a coping, a plinth and (dependent on the height) a string course or two, not only for aesthetic reasons, but also to give stability to the wall and stop rainwater percolating through the body of the masonry. In addition, it is usual to incorporate strengthening piers at regular intervals in the work, the piers also serving to mask any necessary expansion joints. The drawing shows the retainer as a vertical wall but you will often find examples battered back to offer a more effective check to the retained material; additionally relieving arches are often incorporated which can add much to the visual impact of the design, particularly if the face of the wall is vertical and the rear wall of the niches is raked.

The example illustrated was constructed of ¼in balsa sheet, the piers being cut from ½in material, the grain running at right angles to that of the wall itself. Balsa is not much given to warping but it is as well to take reasonable precautions against that possibility.

The structure can be finished as brickwork, rubble stone with ashlar quoins, or completely in cut stone. It depends very much on your personal taste and the area in which your model is located. Of course the counsel of perfection would be to face the whole of the work in modelling clay and detail the stone by hand but if the retaining wall is of considerable length, the operation can become rather tedious and if boredom sets in, the quality of the work can

very easily deteriorate.

I would strongly recommend the products of Faller for this type of operation. This firm offers a whole range of printed and embossed sheets for various forms of stonework and if used with discretion and enlivened with a little shading in water colour, they are most satisfactory. The sheets are available in varying colours representative of sandstone, limestone, etc, and in two thicknesses of card, the lighter being quite adequate when, as in this example, it is backed by balsa.

The introduction of the piers overcomes any problems of face joints in the stone sheet, but care should be exercised to ensure that the bed joints follow through right around the pier. The coping was cut to follow the plan form of the retainer from 0.060in styrene, the upper surface being weathered with fine sandpaper. The string course was fabricated from the ever useful microstrip, the way in which it follows neatly round the projecting piers should be noted.

Where local conditions required it and adequate headroom could be obtained, it was a common practice to form open vaults which could be used for general storage, or occasionally let out to various tradesmen rather in the manner of the timber merchant shown in the drawing. In this case the segmental arch was cut from 0.010in styrene, the voussoirs being touched in with process white to match the remainder of the pointing, before the arch was cut from the sheet with spring bow dividers and fixed in place with a brushful of Mekpak. The fancy keystone is an optional extra!

The inset frontage to Mr Nash's premises was cut from 0.020in Plastiglaze after the glazing bars had been traced on in Humbrol flat white. The fascia was cut from a slip of black Plastikard, the lettering comes from a Blick dry print sheet No BOE 59 in white. The remainder of the detailing, frames and cills, etc, are again cut from microstrip.

The photographs on pages 8 and 36 give an idea of the finished appearance of this particular design at the rear of the goods yard on my layout and hopefully it livens up what could otherwise be rather an uninteresting base to the approach road above it. The stairway was in the nature of an afterthought but in this case it does justify the pedestrian crossing.

Finally the stone embellishments, coping,

The signalbox located in its position on the layout.

The signalbox at Topsham.

The rear elevation. Note 'local colour', estate agents' advertisements.

string course, etc, were touched in with Humbrol No 71, a matt, very pale yellow ochre which gives a good imitation of Portland stone before atmospheric pollution degrades the colour; pollution is something unheard of in the salt spray air of Porthcurno. (They have not heard of a railway there either, but that is another story.)

The retaining wall on the coast near St Just.

Caledonian fish van and six-wheel milk tanks on Porthcurno causeway.

6
Churches

Have you noticed the way in which the English village huddles around its church, with a cluster of red tiled or grey slated roofs, or golden yellow thatch and the church tower soaring above them pointing a finger at Heaven? The rolling landscape is dotted with these cameos, each with its focal point of spire or turreted tower, and no self respecting layout can afford to ignore the visual interest offered by such a composition.

Figure 19 will no doubt be immediately recognised as a much modified Triang 'Model Land' kit. This was an excellent design in its way but the limitations imposed by mass production rather spoiled the relationship of tower with nave and the outline was too bland, lacking the crispness of crocket and pinnacle and the wandering outline of the Gothic style.

The tower was made up in the normal way but

as it was intended to represent a West Country church, a stair turret was an essential addition. This was fabricated from 0.040in styrene with internal diaphragms at intervals to preserve the octagonal shape. The slit windows were originally trefoils but they were modified in the final version. The crenellated top was designed to match the tower, and the flagstaff from the kit was relocated on the turret. The only remaining work to the tower consisted of a little extra emphasis to the corner buttresses, achieved by an additional layer of 0.060in material and the crocketted pinnacles carefully set into the corners of the battlements. These rather make the design I feel and were fabricated from ¼in square balsa, faced with Plastikard to the lower sections. The crocketted terminals were given a coating of 'Das' modelling paste and the crockets themselves formed with the aid of an icing

Figure 19.

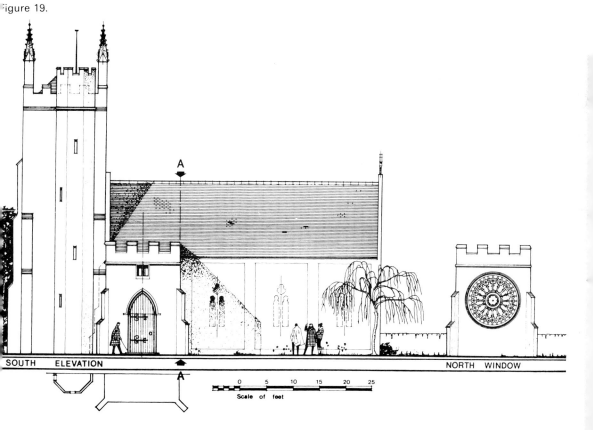

SOUTH ELEVATION   NORTH WINDOW

Scale of feet

0 5 10 15 20 25

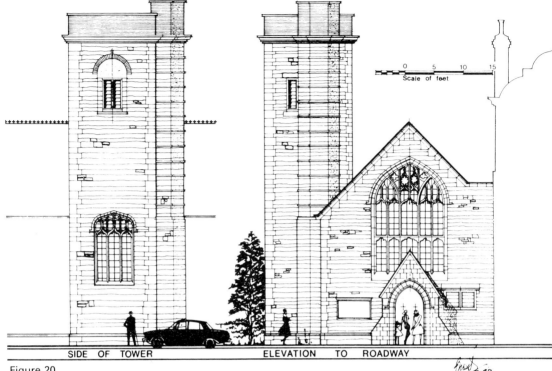

SIDE OF TOWER   ELEVATION TO ROADWAY

Figure 20.

pipette on temporary loan from the kitchen when my wife's attention was elsewhere. The pipette was filled with a charge of thinned down modelling paste and it worked very well. A rather delicate touch is required and the work is simplified if the pinnacle is moistened with Resin W before applying the crockets. It really is worth taking care over this detail as it is such a characteristic feature of this style of building.

As the nave of the Triang model is so unrealistically short, an additional bay was inserted and this took the form of the projecting entrance porch to the south elevation, matched by a small chapel complete with rose window to the north.

These additions were formed from 0.040in styrene sheet, the rose window being cut with spring bow dividers as was the two-centred arch of the entrance doorway. All the doors to the church were cut from sapele veneer, eggshell varnished and with studs, planking and hinge straps indicated in waterproof Indian ink. The tracery of the rose window came from a plastic beer mat from the 'local' thereby saving a considerable amount of detail work. Before being attached to the body of the nave, these additional details were faced up with modelling

compound and finished as rubblestone with cut quoins.

The whole of the completed structure, excluding the roof, was then given a couple of coats of what I call instant stone solution. This is a somewhat peculiar fluid made by dissolving small pieces of plastic sheet in Mekpak until it resembles a thinnish cream. Fine silver sand obtained from a local garden centre is then sieved through a tea strainer and the finer particles shaken into the mixture and thoroughly stirred. This fluid completely disguises the plastic origin of the building and gives a craggy stonelike look and texture to the work. In addition it can be persuaded to flow through an old draughtsman's bow pen to reinforce the effect of coursed rubble stone and to stimulate tuck jointing and the effects of weathering to the stonework of string courses, label mouldings and mullions.

The plastic roof included with the kit was discarded since it was now much too short. New roof slopes were made from 0.040in material faced with squared paper, and after cementing in position, individual roof slates were applied.

Finally the building was finished in a pale creamy grey, weathered to represent limestone.

ELEVATION FACING CATHEDRAL CLOSE

0   10   20   30   40   Scale of feet

Figure 20a.

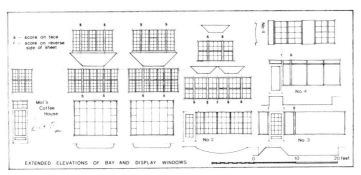

s — score on face
r — score on reverse
side of sheet

Mol's
Coffee
House

No. 4

No 4

No 2   No 3

EXTENDED ELEVATIONS OF BAY AND DISPLAY WINDOWS   0   10   20 feet

Figure 20b.

and the roof was again the inevitable Delabole slate. Let yourself go a little with the application of lichen, mossy patches of damp, aerial visiting cards and the like, painted in water colours when the base coat is completely dry. Our church would be three or four hundred years old and must be finished to look its age.

Figure 20 presents some details of St Martin's church, sited in a corner of the Cathedral Close at Exeter and somewhat overshadowed by its more massive neighbour. I had already modelled the group of buildings which includes the well known Elizabethan half timbered structure known as Mol's Coffee House, details of which are included here (Figure 20a) but it looked unfinished without the church to point a little contrast.

I therefore made a somewhat sketchy survey on a quiet winter morning and the drawings shown are the result. St Martin's is a typical small city church which can be tucked into any corner on the layout. It is a very simple structure except that a little care is required in modelling the tracery of the windows. As I knew that the

The church shown in Figure 19. Note the details of the
trees.

The 'rose' window to the small chapel.

Pick up goods passing St Just village and creek.

model would not be successful unless I could satisfactorily reproduce the bar tracery, this section of the work was tackled first.

A plaster slab was cast against a sheet of glass and the outline of the tracery drawn on it. The design was then cut and scraped away as described in an earlier chapter and finally the window was cast in melted solder. This was repeated for each window with the exception of the louvred openings to the belfry and proved very successful.

The remainder of the model was formed of 0.040in styrene sheet, faced up with 'Das' modelling clay and finished as uncoursed rubble with cut quoins. The prototype finish is in Heavitree stone, a coarse red Devon sandstone which due to its soft and open texture, weathers very badly.

The topmost stage of the tower is in faced brickwork and the combination of the brick parapet with the repeated projecting strings on the stair turret and the heavy moulding above the belfry windows is full of character to say the least. We are not looking for purity of style, but our models should reflect reality and St Martin's is certain to do that.

The windows of the church are unusual in that they are equipped with wrought iron glazing bars which give a slightly domestic quality to the fenestration, although the stained glass is fabricated using lead cames in the ecclesiastical manner.

How much detail you introduce into the windows is a matter of personal taste. It is possible to take colour transparencies of the original and mount them behind the bar tracery if you are seeking absolute fidelity to the prototype.

I have found that a satisfactory effect can be achieved by indicating the lead cames with closely spaced lines drawn in waterproof Indian ink on the face of the glazing. The coloured glass is then drawn in somewhat thinned down Humbrol colours applied to the rear of the window. Subdued lighting within the body of the church will give sparkle to the leaded lights and the night effect is very convincing.

Red Devon Sandstone (Heavitree stone, Pocombe stone and so forth) can be reproduced most easily by first covering the stonework with an all over coating of Humbrol 26 let down with a little matt white; when it is completely dry, the elevations are washed over with tints of Indian Red, Burnt Sienna and Raw Umber water

St Martin's with Mol's Coffee House, a familiar view facing Exeter cathedral.

colour. The mottled effect conveyed by mixing the media gives a pleasing finish.

The roof is slated in the usual way, set down behind the gables, and the ridge can be fabricated by snippets from the ornamental railings available from the Scale Link Co, set in position with a line of microstrip on either side.

A view of the original in Exeter.

7
Inns

As my layout is quite modest in size, housed in the smallest bedroom in the house, my friends pretend to see a deep psychological significance in the number of licensed premises which appear on the model. Actually there are only three and as inns and public houses are usually of such outstanding architectural interest, they simply cry out to be modelled; at least that is my explanation and I am sticking to it!

Figures 21 and 22 owe their inspiration to an inn on the edge of Romney Marsh (The White Hart at Newenden) and is based on a pencil sketch made many years ago with very few dimensions. The front elevation is reasonably accurate, or it was at the time; the passing years may have had their effect and it is a long time since I was in that area. The rear elevation is pure conjecture but reasonably in character with the design as a whole.

The combination of white painted weather

Figure 21.

FRONT   ELEVATION

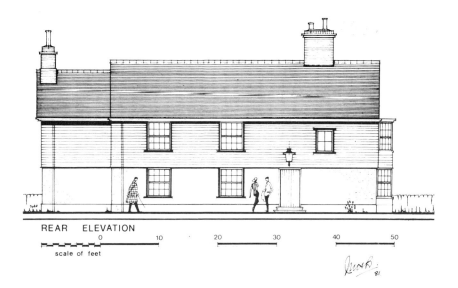

REAR   ELEVATION

scale of feet

extended elevation of
two storey bay window

Figure 22.   ELEVATIONS   OF   GABLES

boarding to the first floor and rendering to the ground floor is visually most attractive especially with the warm russet tones of the hand made tiles to the roof. Of course the windows are a bit of a hotch potch, mainly Georgian in flavour but they do make a lively composition.

The model was constructed largely from 0.040in styrene sheet, the weather boards being cut from postcard and separately applied. Do not attempt to go from end to end of the building with one board, transport problems alone would have limited the maximum length to about 12ft or so. The window frames project slightly at the first floor to provide a stop to the boarding, the frames being picked out in black,

the sashes and glazing bars in white. Note the bell mouth profile of the lowermost boards; this is a characteristic feature of this form of construction and should be followed with care.

There is a slight break in the front elevation indicating a later addition (further confirmed by the drop in the roof) but the projection is very small, no more than 4½in and the eaves run through.

Note the compound chimney, the lamps over the entrance doors and (although they do not show all that well on the photographs) the brass kicking plates to the doors, which are again of wood veneer, eggshell varnished and lined in Indian ink. The kicking plates are formed of

Figure 23.

ELEVATION   FACING   RIVER   EXE

Scale of feet
0   10   20   30   40   50   60

The inn shown in Figures 21 and 22.

brass foil Sellotape, worth keeping in stock as it makes excellent brass boiler bands, professional nameplates, letter boxes, etc, and is a most useful product.

Incidentally it is worth looking out for brewer's trade signs and motifs which are very characteristic and can often be cut from advertisements in the Sunday colour supplements. They carry much conviction when carefully mounted on the model but do not use Mekpak as an adhesive for this purpose. The fluid causes the printer's ink to run very badly and spoil the illustration. Mount them in position with Uhu or clear Bostick.

Figure 23 was prepared by calculating the dimensions from photographs in the manner already described in detail in Chapter 1. It shows the Passage Inn at Topsham on the River Exe, a building of mediaeval foundation but much altered over the years by the insertion of Georgian type windows, slate hanging to the double gable and a classical door casing complete with pediment.

The slate hanging covers a jettied timber frame, that is a first floor which overhangs the ground by a foot or more and the gables at second floor level project again, taking their bearing from a very heavy cornice, no doubt introduced at the same time as the pedimented entrance door. The double pitch of the roof on the left of the drawing is unusual and forms an interesting contrast to the main structure.

The model was constructed largely from styrene sheet, the tile hanging being applied on a backing of squared paper to preserve the regularity of the courses. The entrance doors and shutters were cut from wood veneer finished with eggshell varnish, the details being drawn in as described before. Note the tarred plinth which gave some protection from rising moisture, damp proof courses being conspicuous by their absence in buildings of this age.

Apart from the slate hanging, the remainder of the elevations on the prototype are finished in sand and cement rendering, relatively easily simulated on the model by a couple of coats of the stone solution already referred to and then painted over in flat white paint. To avoid any hint of monotony in the colouring, it is advisable to introduce a little yellow ochre into the white, and grade the tone down to pavement level as in nature there is no such thing as a perfectly flat colour. Every tone is affected to some degree by its surroundings, the sunlight on the roadway reflects into the lower part of the walls lightening their colour, the lower part of the chimney

The rear elevation of the inn (sunshine after showers).

A close up of the slate hanging and the entrance pediment.

Note the strap hinges to the shutters and the window cleaner.

The Globe Hotel shown in Figure 24.

Figure 24.

THE GLOBE HOTEL

DEVENISH ALES

ELEVATION TO ROADWAY

END ELEVATION

0 5 10 15 20 25
Scale of feet

stacks would be illuminated by sunlight reflected off the roofing slates and therefore the brickwork would appear to be darker at the top especially seen against the azure blue of the Devon sky. The final impact of any model depends very much on its colouring and time spent in careful observation of the colours of nature and their effect on man made structures, will pay a handsome dividend in added realism and greater visual impact in the model.

Incidentally, you will notice that the chimney stacks are finished in faced brickwork despite the rendering of the remainder of the structure. This is almost invariably the case as the heat of the flue gases would cause the rendering to spall away in a very short period of time.

Figure 24, The Globe Hotel, is based on an original, again at Topsham, which incidentally is a veritable treasure house of architectural gems and well worth a visit when next you come to the West Country on holiday. A combination of factors including an inadequate drainage system have militated against the machinations of the dreaded developer and a very large part of this little estuary town remains untouched by the tasteless hands of commercialism.

The model was made largely from 0.040in styrene sheet but for a change the rendering was represented by medium grade sandpaper attached to the elevations quite easily with a wash of solvent and placed in a heavy book overnight to ensure flat drying. The sandpaper was left in its natural colour and looks most

attractive in contrast with the white reveals and framing of the sash windows.

I have indicated a pantiled roof set down behind a parapet which is quite easy to model and makes a pleasant change in the general roofscape of my layout but regrettably is not true to the prototype; it is, if you like, a bit of artist's licence. The roof slopes were coated with a thin and even layer of modelling clay and then the pantiles were pressed into the plastic surface using the butt end of an ordinary writing nib reversed in its holder.

When the various sections of the roof were completely hard and dry, they were assembled with Uhu and the ridge and hip tiles modelled by rolling out a thin sausage of modelling clay, pressing into position, and then impressing the individual tiles, again with the aid of the nib, the hips being finished in the manner of 'Granny bonnets'.

The colouring of the roof gave me a lot of pleasure as on a base coat of mid Indian Red with touches of vermilion it was possible using the dry brush technique to attain a really convincing effect with relatively little effort.

The cornice was fabricated from Microstrip and the details around the entrance door, the canopy, consoles and fascia were made of the same material. The lettering attached to the parapet above the cornice was made up from plastic letters by Faller and obtained from my local model shop. They were finished in gold enamel, painted before they were mounted in position, again with Uhu. Whatever you do, do not try to paint them in situ, as the slightest slip with the brush and the gold enamel flashes into the sandpaper backing as if it were blotting paper and you are faced with a difficult repair job. If you look carefully at the photograph you will see where I made just such a repair. Like the Vicar of Bray, don't do as I do, do as I say, for there is no point in two of us making the same mistakes.

The hanging sign I made from brass shim to represent the scrollwork of wrought iron. It was a fiddling job but the model was made before the excellent products of Scale Link appeared on the market. My later work invariably makes use of their chemically etched frets with a great improvement to the finish.

As you may have inferred, I have taken a few liberties with the prototype to which it bears only a passing resemblance, but the model, possibly due to the mixture of materials and the general proportions, is always a favourite with visitors when some of my later and more accurate representations go almost unnoticed. There is a moral in this somewhere.

8
Country Town Shops and Houses

With one or two exceptions, most towns and villages in the United Kingdom are of very ancient foundation, often harking back to the Roman era, and the study of their development is a fascinating pastime. Up to and including mediaeval times, the hamlet developed as a series of detached dwellings clustering around the Church, or huddling for protection close to the fortified castle of the Squire. But as the population increased and a more stable and prosperous community developed, the spaces between adjoining houses were filled in, half timbered façades were cloaked with a Georgian front and with the coming of the industrial revolution, the terrace house became possibly the most characteristic aspect of the urban scene.

Figure 25 sets out the salient features of a Georgian terrace which can be as lengthy as the modeller desires to fit in with the requirements of the layout. The construction of the model is quite straightforward, the elevations being cut from 0.040in styrene in the manner described on page 28, that is by scoring lines across the sheet of plastic at the heads and cills of the windows and then from eaves to ground on the line of the window reveals. The plastic can then be broken up, snapping cleanly on the scored lines and then reassembled leaving the window apertures accurately in line both horizontally and vertically.

The details of the cornice, the string course, the balconies and the entrance door cases were worked up in microstrip, the balustrades to the first floor balconies being formed from Plasti-glaze with the balusters drawn on the transparent material in matt white paint using a ruling pen. The finished effect can be judged from the photographs on page 70.

The mansard roofs for the terrace were formed as separate units and when completely finished with slating in place, were set in position between the projecting party walls which rise above the roof to offer a fire check in conformity with the building regulations then in force. Do not attempt to attach the dormer windows to the raking face of the mansard. They are modelled as separate little boxes with glazed front and leaded cheeks and take their bearing from a false flat roof just below the cornice level. This is the only way to ensure that the dormers are truly vertical and the same

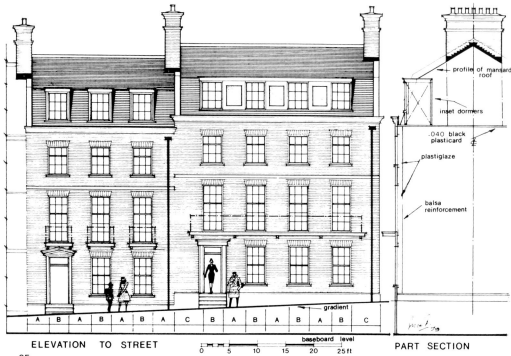

profile of mansard roof

inset dormers

.040 black plasticard

plastiglaze

balsa reinforcement

ELEVATION TO STREET

gradient

baseboard level

0   5   10   15   20   25 ft

PART SECTION

A B A B A B A C B A B A B A B C

Figure 25.

comment applies to the chimney stacks which pass through the roof and are firmly cemented to the party walls.

The visual impact of the terrace depends for its success on the regular repetition of the individual units but it is worth trying to introduce a little variety into the work by treating the door casings in differing ways, one with a pediment, another with a canopy supported by consoles; similarly the balconies and dormers may differ as is shown on the drawing, and I hope brought out in the photographs.

It is worth noting that this paricular terrace on my layout faces a roadway with quite a severe gradient. On sites of this nature it is important that the model is taken down to the level of the baseboard proper and this is indicated on the sketch. It cannot be overstressed that the eye has an amazing facility to note immediately any variation in verticality on the model, so make sure that your walls are truly vertical and this comment applies with equal force to such details as signals and telegraph poles. Check them for truth from all angles before finally cementing them in position. A small steel square is very useful for this work but a set square is equally valuable.

The façades of the terrace are finished in faced brickwork the flat arches being drawn in with a brown felt tip pen. The roofs were always in slate, either Welsh (dark purple blue) Delabole (grey white with greenish overtones) or imported from Normandy (chalky grey, much lighter in tone).

The rainwater fallpipes were usually square in section and connected with a hopper head on the level of the parapet gutter. They are made from scraps of plastic rod, painted a dark matt grey before being fixed to the facades with Uhu.

Figure 26 deals with the range of dwellings positioned immediately alongside the Georgian terrace in 'Station Road' forming the main access to the goods depot at Porthcurno. It is an interesting mixture based yet again on a former prototype at Topsham near Exeter. Unfortunately the original was destroyed by fire some little time ago and has been rebuilt to an entirely different design.

The model utilises a variety of materials in its construction, the antique shop and 'Station Road Stores' being cast in plaster in the manner described in Chapter 4. This was the easiest solution in coping with the projections of the jettied gable of the former and the coursed rubble stone facing of the latter.

The model is slightly curved on plan following

The Georgian terrace shown in Figure 25.

the line of the carriageway so the drawing is an extended elevation to avoid the distortion caused by flat perspective.

The remainder of the model was formed in 0.040in Plastikard, the joint between plaster and

plastic being effected with Uhu after giving the interfaces a priming coat of adhesive and allowing them to dry before completing the work.

The variety of facings on the prototype was truly amazing and for this reason it makes a

Figure 26.

| 0 | 5 | 10 | 15 | 20 | 25 | 30 | Scale of feet | Datum Level 〕 |

ELEVATION TO STATION ROAD

MB · 1981·

A close up detail of the balconies and entrances.

good and interesting model. The rubble stonework was finished as Beerstone, a creamy white, and all the slating as Delabole. The sand and cement render to the antique shop received a wash of warm process white, while the rendering to the double gables of 'The Cabin' was coloured a pinkish shade which although quite traditional in the South West I am not at all sure

about it on the model. When the spirit is willing I may repaint it in white and this I would advise you to do, as there is quite enough variety on this model without overdoing it.

The Tudor chimney with linked octagonal flues was made quite simply by cutting three lengths from the stem of a ballpoint pen which had the required shape, covering them with

Figure 27.

ELEVATION TO VILLAGE STREET

0   5   10   15   20   25
Scale of feet

SIDE   ELEVATION

G FIDDLER

ANTIQUES

WATCH & CLOCK REPAIRS

CAR PARK

MB 1981

brickpaper and gluing the flues to each other and then to the rectangular base with its projecting cap. Do not omit the simple dentilled cornice to the living quarters of the antique shop. It makes a pleasing foil to the slate hanging.

Figure 27 shows rather an attractive little village shop with attached living accommodation and exhibits some of those eccentricities of the local builder which are always worth looking out for.

The original fabric was obviously mediaeval as the jettied frontage gives evidence of a half timbered origin. Some modifications were carried out in Georgian times judging by the first floor windows but the bays at ground level can only be Victorian. The little balcony, complete with French windows, is an interesting detail.

The wandering outline of the external chimney with the bargeboards split by the brickwork of the stack is the feature which first caught my eye. It comes up very well on the model, particularly with the lettering to the gable applied in dry print and improved a little with the pen to reduce the regularity of the sign.

The model is basically of Plastikard, with in this case, a russet tiled roof. The elevations are rendered in a pale ochre shade, Humbrol 83 let

down with plenty of white. Notice the rather heavy moulding at the base of the first floor overhang. This detail together with the fascia and entrance door to the little shop were finished in Humbrol 98, a delightful flat sepia colour which exactly catches the effect of exposed half timbering. Vary the shades a little by running the merest flick of a contrasting colour into the wash while it is still wet.

You can let yourself go a little on the tiled roof, which is basically a light indian red (Humbrol 70) but with odd tiles picked out in vermilion and indications of moss and lichen, particularly around the chimney stacks. The half round ridge tiles were made from the insulating sleeve of ordinary domestic wiring. The copper conductor was carefully drawn out and put on one side for use in making the fall-pipes, and then the resulting plastic tube was carefully slit down one side with the modelling knife, cut into small sections, and after opening up the cut with the back of the blade, the miniature ridge tiles were cemented in position on the ridge with the ever useful Uhu. The rather untidy pointing of the joints is indicated with a touch of light grey paint.

Figure 28 is another Devon riverside dwelling showing strong Dutch influence, particularly in

Figure 28.

WEST ELEVATION SOUTH ELEVATION

Extended elevation of Bow Window

0   10   20   30
Scale of feet.

1980.

The village shop shown in Figure 27.

the somewhat elaborate curves of the gable. In the heyday of the wool trade there was considerable traffic between the ports of the South West and Holland, the ships returning to Britain often in ballast, the ballast most usually being Dutch bricks. This accounts for the very early development of brick-built dwellings along the Devon rivers and estuaries when the remainder of the county was mainly cob and thatch.

The model is straightforward made generally from 0.040in styrene, the elevations being rendered with the exception of the external stack to the gable which is in faced brickwork. Note the horizontally sliding shutters, a typical Devon feature, contained between an upper moulding and the cill. The louvred shutters can be effectively modelled in thick transparent plastic, the rear of the sheet being painted a dull grey, the front being lined out in pale green with a draughtsman's bow pen to indicate the separate louvres. The eye (and the camera) are completely deceived, the shadows on the face of the sheet being cast on the mid grey rear in a truly convincing manner. Attach the shutters to the model with double sided Sellotape since if a liquid adhesive if used, the rear coating of paint will be damaged and the effect ruined.

The roof is tiled and set down behind the upper parapet, seating onto a false flat of 0.030in black Plastikard at the level of the window heads. I have indicated by a dotted line, the position of the roof slopes behind the gables which are finished with a coping in the normal manner.

The bow window is a Regency addition and is fabricated from Plastiglaze, the sashes being lined out in matt white. The transparent material was then taped to a metal pill box which was filled with very hot water to mould the glazing to the required curve. Notice that the entrance door is set within a deeply recessed porch which is better formed as a complete unit before being cemented in position.

The stucco finish was painted in pale yellow ochre shaded off to the base with matt white, all the mouldings being white and formed from the indispensable microstrip.

Figure 29 sets out the details of the cottage immediately adjacent to the Passage Inn at Topsham, a hostelry already dealt with in a previous chapter. The cottage itself is somewhat of a mongrel of doubtful ancestry but such is the perversity of human nature, that when the Passage Inn appeared in *Railway Modeller*

Figure 29.

ELEVATION TO ROAD   Feet   0 5 10 15 20   GABLE END

some little time ago, I received several requests for details of this cottage which has nothing like the architectural quality of the inn. Here it is in all its Victorian remodelled splendour. It makes a good model, the cantilevered bays at first floor level and the porch protecting the entrance ensuring plenty of visual interest.

The bays were folded up from plastiglaze, the render coating being taken right across the

section beneath the cills. The hipped and leaded bay roofs were cut from obechi and sanded to a sharp outline. Notice that the house eaves carry over the bay heads.

The ground floor windows have quite a significant architrave brought out in microstrip which forms a stop for the sand and cement render coat. Incidentally it is worth taking trouble to form the bell mouth drip to the projecting bays; it is a very typical detail and the

A detail of the chimney stack and the mouldings of the side gable.

The cottage shown in Figure 29.

A view of the original cottage.

The group shown in Figures 30 and 31 under construction. Note the oriel window.

The effect of the shutters and the 'stone' paint.

The Georgian façade finished as 'stucco' with the stone paint.

A close up of the classical entrance. The wall texture is well brought out. Note the letter plate of brass foil sellotape.

ELEVATION TO ROADWAY

Scale of feet
0 5 10 15 20

Figure 30.

correct way of terminating the projection. The slated roof is Delabole finished with a half round clay ridge tile which forms a pleasing contrast. The porch was modelled in styrene sheet, the supporting posts and the timbering to the simplified king post truss, a somewhat prominent feature of the structure, being framed up in obechi strip. The ridge tiles to the porch roof on the prototype are quite an elaborate pattern with perforated upstands, brought out in the photograph on page 74.

The whole of the timbering was painted white as were the frames and sashes of the windows, contrasting with the render coat which was treated with a graded wash of yellow ochre shading down to the base.

The cottage is set back from the roadway with a paved forecourt, decorated with shrubs, some in tubs, but the majority planted in little gaps in the stone slabs. It is worth taking a little time over this mini-horticulture; it seems to settle the model very nicely into the landscape and makes a pleasant diversion from the somewhat formal discipline of miniature building construction.

The final examples offered in this chapter and shown in Figures 30 and 31 are a composite group connected at ground level by a rubble stone wall pierced by a common entrance doorway.

Figure 30 is actually of two dwellings in widely differing styles, the house on the left hand side being obviously of Georgian foundation verging on Regency, judging by the windows and the horizontal sliding shutters which we have come across in a previous example, and which are modelled in exactly the same way. I have made a few alterations in the drawing to adapt the model to its place on my layout so it is not a completely accurate copy of the original but I have been careful to preserve the general style.

The house to the right on the same drawing exhibits two interesting features, the oriel window at the first floor and the little observatory or penthouse built on the flat roof. The property was modernized in comparatively modern times with quite a degree of good taste I feel.

The external finish is in rubble stone which forms a pleasant contrast to the sand and cement rendering of its neighbour, the stone being a curious amalgam of red sandstone with bits of limestone worked into the courses. I strongly suspect that a decaying sea wall on the estuary was used as a 'quarry' for much of the work.

The dominant feature of the design, the oriel window was folded up from Plastiglaze insofar as the sashes are concerned, the hipped and

ELEVATION TO ROADWAY　　　　　　　　　　　　　　　GABLE END

0　5　10　15　20　25

Scale of feet

Figure 31.

leaded roof and the rather subtle curved support below the cill being shaped up from block balsa. They were then given a skim coat of Das modelling clay, primarily to fill the grain of the wood but also to follow more closely the curves of the prototype.

Figure 31 is a straightforward Georgian house with Victorian overtones. Its proportions are very satisfying, despite the rather odd quirk of the little cottage on the right of the façade under a common cornice. Originally the property must have been two separate dwellings although I believe at the present time, they are under the same ownership.

It is interesting to note the manner in which the cornice returns on the gable end (shades of the Queen Anne front and Mary Anne behind), an arrangement often encountered. Incidentally a lot of these old houses have quite a tale to tell if you walk around them. Very often you will come across a half timbered structure of mediaeval foundation at the rear of a dwelling which sports a Georgian or Regency street frontage. Keeping up with the Jones's is an old established pastime!

The photographs on page 75 show sections of this group under construction and demonstrate the application of various finishes to the flat facades before they are joined to form the finished model. You will notice that the rubble stone is quite adequately copied in Das modelling paste applied to a 0.040in styrene sheet backing. It is important to form a key for this coating by heavily scoring the plastic sheet before applying the paste. The stone texture was copied using a scrap piece of plastic as a modelling tool to impress the joints in a random manner. A few strokes of the modelling knife indicated the quoins. The window apertures are framed around with microstrip before the modelling paste is applied, to ensure a clean finish to the reveals. Of course the glazing is not fixed in position before all this structural work is complete, the Das thoroughly hard and the window reveals painted.

When the various façades are joined one to the other to form the finished building, it will be necessary to make good to the quoins with modelling clay, running the courses through with the knife and, using plenty of water on the blade, smoothing the corners to a sharp and true angle.

9

Industrial and Public Buildings

Factories and warehouses, office blocks and public halls have one thing in common, a large and often massive scale which, unless the model is relegated to a painted image on the back scene, can be difficult to assimilate into the miniature landscape.

Thus it pays to keep an eye open for suitable examples which can be reproduced without becoming over dominant, and at the same time will provide a reason for the traffic arriving at your goods yard.

Figures 32 and 33 are based upon the Maltings at Bishops Stortford, an attractive early Victorian building of almost domestic scale as is evidenced by the easy way in which the malting floors run into the adjacent dwelling house and all contained under a pleasant slated roof.

The white weatherboarding and warm brickwork are a happy combination, the cantilevered loading bay being carried on ornamental brackets obtained from one of the chemically etched sheets produced by Scale Link Ltd. It will be noted that the ventilation openings to the drying

floors are filled with louvres, indicated on the model by white lining on Plastiglaze and framed around in microstrip.

The external brick piers are not present on the prototype but I have introduced them on the design to lend a little more interest to what would otherwise be a rather uninteresting stretch of walling. They were applied separately after they had been faced with an appropriate brick finish (in this case Superquick D1 red brick) and were attached in position with Uhu. The cills, string courses and other details were made from microstrip while the flat arches over windows, doors and vents were simply picked out on the brick face with a brown felt tip pen. When this was dry, the separate voussoirs were drawn on in Humbrol No 70 using a draughtsman's pen, and this so enlivened the texture of the work that I introduced random stretchers in the same colour over the whole façade. The criticism often levelled at printed brickpaper is its lack of surface texture but this can be easily remedied by laying the sheet over a piece of

Figure 32.

ft. [scale bar] 0   10   20   30   ELEVATION TO QUAY.

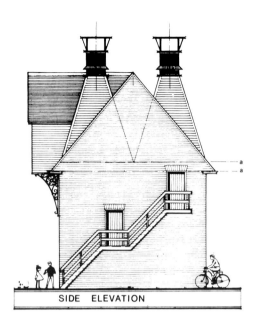

Figure 33.

SIDE ELEVATION

coarse sand paper and pressing all over the surface with the heel of the hand before mounting onto the plastic sheet. In a similar fashion a little additional detailing with matt paint in the manner already suggested will be found to be a great improvement.

The pyramidical roofs to the kilns require a degree of care as they are such a dominant element of the design. The kiln roofs are better completely formed and mounted in position before the main roof slopes are cut to fit around them. The work will be found easier if tackled in this way.

The kerbs and aprons of the caps are formed in a styrene, the terminal flue and wrought iron cover plate on its little angular stays can be soldered up from a slip of tinplate with copper wire braces to the angles. Originally I fabricated these features completely in Plastikard but they are so prone to accidental damage from sleeve cuffs reaching over the layout that I eventually replaced them in metal.

As can be seen from the photographs, my Maltings are situated on a quay side, a somewhat unlikely location perhaps, but that is where my industrial zone is sited. Some aspects of marine engineering in general and quays in particular should be noted. The sea wall where it is serving a possible loading area is usually vertical, constructed of heavy and massive stone blocks with a suitable coping at the head. The face is almost invariably protected by heavy

timber balks which save the masonry from damage when ships are docked and tied up alongside. Note from the photographs the way in which the timbering is arranged as it is very easy to make a mistake in this respect. The stringers are first bolted to the face of the stonework, the vertical timbers then being fixed to the face of the strings. My model quay sports a Faller embossed stone facing (sheet No 552/6); the timbering is obechi strip finished with dark oak stain. The completed model was toned down with water colour in slimy greens and browns, with a few rusty ring bolts and access ladders for added interest.

Water I find is best represented by clear perspex sheet backed with a sheet of dark brown poster paper with a patch of weed here and there graded to a darker green as the dock gets deeper.

A good wave effect can be achieved by the use of 'cling film', well crumpled between the hands, then straightened out and pressed into contact with the surface of the perspex, in a rather hit and miss fashion. The flow of the water is simulated by brushing the hand along the cling film, when it forms ripples following the direction of the movement. The method is rather difficult to describe in words but if you study the photograph on page 81 you will rapidly get the hang of it. Of course this procedure has a great advantage in that if you are dissatisfied with the effect, the film can be

A GWR 2–6–2T runs light down the quay. Note the cling film water treatment.

readily stripped off and remodelled until success is achieved. Similarly if the 'water' becomes somewhat dusty after a period of time, it is the work of only a few minutes to reform the waves with a new sheet of film.

It might be thought that mirror glass would be the best solution for the reproduction of water but I have never found this to be so. The reflected image is rather too hard and mechanical and because of the silvered backing, the thickness of the glass becomes very obvious, resulting in a double line to the reflection, particularly when viewed obliquely.

The working surface of the quay is normally finished in cobblestones or paviors and for this purpose I like the effect given by Faller embossed cobbles or pavé. It is very convincing and even includes manhole covers and drainage channels. If you wish to set railway track into the road surface, it is necessary to glue the embossed card to mounting board of a suitable thickness to bring the combination to the same height as the head of the rail. Allow an adequate space inside the rail edges for the wheel flanges. When the work is completed, run an old wagon several times up and down the track with moderate hand pressure to clear any debris out of the flangeway, pressing down any protruding slips of card, which could interfere with current collection to the locomotive driving wheels.

You will find all this work more than justified when you see your battered pannier tank or elderly prairie wandering down the quay with a few wagons for the maltings, or picking up one or two fish vans from the drifters fresh in on the morning tide. The Great Western seemed to be wedded to the sea like the Doge of Venice and your model will reproduce a sight now only to be seen I think at one place in the UK – Kingswear, on the estuary of the Dart. It is of such stuff that dreams are made of.

Wherever men go down to the sea in ships, there you will find a Customs Collector eagerly awaiting their return, pencil poised, coffers open ready to receive the fruits of other men's labours. And these officials were housed in considerable style, particularly in the South West, as witness the Custom House on the quay at Exeter shown in Figures 34 and 35.

This is a fairly well known example as it appeared many times in *The Onedin Line*, the long running television serial where it masqueraded as the Shipping Exchange in Liverpool. The façade facing the river is a particularly attractive example of late Georgian work with

Local pick up goods passing the Custom House.

considerable Dutch influence, not surprising in view of the trading links between the two countries during the wool era. The detailing of the arcade at ground level is perhaps a little heavy, and the block treatment of the capitals to the pilasters can only be said to be virile as they are innocent of any refinement of moulding, but they are all the easier to reproduce.

The model was constructed in Plastikard with red facing brick tinted down with water colour to contrast with the limestone facings to the general fenestration. The extension to the right of the elevation is obviously later work judging by the simplified treatment to the architraves and the omission of the base moulding to the dentilled cornice. The string course also is continued in brickwork, rather than stone.

Due to the complications of the roof and in particular the necessity to make a satisfactory job of the cornice and the pediment, the building was constructed in two separate sections, the roof fitting over the base like a lid. The body of the model was constructed in 0.040in styrene, and as the structure is quite large, balsa wood floors were inserted mainly as an insurance against the possibility of warping. Remember to perforate the internal floors and partitions to allow solvent fumes to escape as the work dries out.

The brickpaper was carried right over each façade, the stone decorations being attached with a brushful of Mekpak to the face of the work when the brickwork was completely dry. The arches to the arcade were cut with bow dividers from 0.020in material, the heads of the ground floor windows being formed to follow the curve of the stone. The pilasters, string course and stone quoins were cut from 0.030in styrene, the bed joints of the quoins being slightly chamfered with an emery board to emphasise the slight rustication of the prototype. It is prudent to have a dry run with the quoins before finally cementing them into place to ensure that the stones fit neatly between the cornice and the string course, and between the latter and the ground.

The work to the roof is based upon a sheet of 0.060in styrene which forms the main fascia, its edges being brought to a smooth face, the dentils being attached to the soffit, care being taken to keep any adhesive away from the mouldings. The drawing indicates the manner in which the crowning mouldings break away from the cornice and follow around the peri-

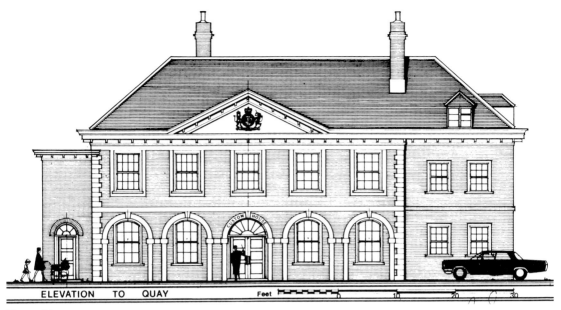

Figure 34.

Figure 35.

meter of the pediment. The detail should be followed carefully in this respect as it is typical of the style. Despite its relatively low pitch (26 degrees) the pediment boasts a slated roof, the slates being mitred neatly to a leaded valley gutter at the junction with the main pitch. Much of this detail is brought out reasonably clearly in the photograph on page 82 but I must confess that this detail shows a slight error which I have perpetrated on the model. The lower face of the

dentils contained within the pediment should be cut to rake to the same angle and not finished square at the base. It is only a small point but one worth watching.

The little dormers are worth modelling carefully as they add much interest to quite a large roof. The hips to these features are slated with a lead roll to the ridge and lead sheet to the side cheeks. You will notice that the dormer windows feature side hung casements and not the

Detail of the hip. Note the treatment of the dentils and the dormer window.

box sashes on the remainder of the building. The arrangement of the glazing bars is also quite different, all indicative of a later addition not quite in harmony with the original design. You will find it more convincing to model some of the windows in the open position and when you do so it is worth drawing the glazing bars on the back as well as the front of the Plastiglaze and running a brushful of white down the exposed edges of the glazing. The prototype sashes would be about 1½in or 2in in thickness, well represented by 0.020in transparent sheet.

The work was completed by the provision of the royal coat of arms in the centre of the pediment. This was copied from the royal appointment panel on a biscuit box, mounted on 0.020in styrene and fixed in position so that the shield sloped slightly forward. You may be able to find an acceptable design ready printed and of a suitable size by keeping an eye on the packaging of the weekly groceries, but the coat of arms is not difficult to draw and provided you use plenty of vermilion red and gold enamel, it provides an eye catching focal point to the whole design.

10
Backgrounds and Scenic Details

An important aspect of modelling buildings is the setting in which they are situated. One of the more surprising aspects of the work is the way in which the models seem to increase in weight as more details are added and the landscaping is completed. It is for that reason that I have advocated the use of lightweight framing (balsa and the like) wherever possible and similarly the contours of the basework can be worked up most conveniently in expanded polystyrene provided it is not required to carry any significant weight and is not subjected to any stress.

On baseboards generally, they are easily framed up from 2in × 1in planed softwood with, in the case of model railway layouts, a solid covering only in those locations where the track is to be laid. The remainder of the area can be left with the framing exposed in the open top manner of construction, filling in the contours with expanded aluminium netting before finally covering with either papier maché or plaster impregnated open weave material sold under a variety of trade names, Modroc being one well known brand. The actual base upon which your model building is to be sited must be level and in this respect if will be found convenient to plot the location of each structure on the baseboard,

and arrange a little plateau of expanded polystyrene (most easily made from scrap ceiling tiles) to receive the model. As I mentioned previously you will find it a great advantage to be able to remove the individual models for necessary repairs which can then be carried out in comfort on your workboard.

Even if your model layout is intended to be permanent, you will be well advised to limit the size of each individual board to a figure not exceeding 4ft × 2ft. This is the maximum size that can be handled with relative ease and transported in the average hatchback should you wish to exhibit your work in the future. I have found it a good plan to arrange a sub-base of 3in × 2in bearers, plugged and screwed to the walls of the railway room, upon which the separate baseboard panels can be supported and located accurately, one to the other with either steel dowels or flap back hinges with the pin removed. In common with many enthusiasts, I started my first model railway on a solid baseboard formed of one panel of chipboard of the maximum dimensions available which was then 8ft × 4ft. By virtue of its size, this had to be arranged with one long edge against the wall, and as is the natural order of things, derailments

The Cornish coast in photographs.

Backscene in pastels.

always took place at the far side of the board, tight up against the wall. Straining over a span of 4ft to replace rolling stock on the track is not an exercise to be undertaken lightly, and moreover it places any scenic details in the immediate foreground in very serious danger. Thus if baseboards wider than 2ft are absolutely essential to your plan, arrange for removable access panels in strategically planned locations.

You will find it an advantage, by the way, to set your model buildings slightly down into the landscape where they do not immediately abut an area of paving. This will enable the horticultural work to be carried right up to the walls, and obviate that unprototypical black line which appears at the base of so many models.

The actual surfacing of the layout depends very much upon the type of vegetation you are reproducing. For general grassland I find a satisfactory effect can be obtained by giving the contours a coat of sticky green gloss paint and then immediately applying a sprinkling of the scenic scatter material, meadow grass, moorland grass, light earth, etc., readily obtainable from any model shop. When this has dried

Dean goods passing St Just.

vacuum off the surplus for re-use and then for a final touch of super detail, spray a little Noch 'Streugras' from one of their puffer bottles in random patches to give variety of colour and texture. The action of puffing the flock from the plastic bottle imparts an electrical charge to each particle with the effect that the little blades of grass stand up from the base in quite an astonishing way.

Suburban lawns are better represented by almond green felt obtainable from a craft shop. Before fixing it in position on the model, remember to indicate the stripes left by the mower with a slightly deeper line of green at regular intervals. I find that thinned down green ink gives the right effect.

The plastic foam material marketed by Hammant & Morgan and sold under the trade name of 'Woodland Scenics' has really revolutionised the manufacture of model trees. It consists of very fine particles of variously coloured foam connected by a network of fine hair, and if used with discretion it is capable of reproducing practically any type of tree.

The method consists of selecting suitable twigs, either from the garden or the nearest patch of woodland, trimming them to an accept-

© MH Bradley. 1980.

able size and shape and then mounting little clusters of rubberized horse hair (John Piper Accessories Ltd) to indicate the finer branches and twigs. This base is then sprayed a dark greyish brown and when dry the foliage is attached with dabs of Resin W adhesive, using a light touch and spreading the plastic material well out so that the separate clusters of leaves appear natural and free. Woodland Scenics foliage is obtainable in a variety of colours from spring green to a highly effective autumnal tint and in my opinion provides the ideal solution to this most difficult of modelling enterprises. The photographs on pages 45 and 58 illustrate trees made in this way and while I do not hold them up as masterpieces of model horticulture, hopefully they are more than usually convincing for work of this type.

Prairies in tandem.

If you would like a little further variety, John Piper offers a range of hand-made trees in several styles, the larger conifers in dark green being I think the most effective. They are skilfully made on the old flue brush principle and are very acceptable, although prices reflect the care taken in their manufacture. They make an ideal present so a hint dropped at Christmas or some other appropriate time may not come amiss.

There are also ranges of plastic trees of continental manufacture readily available in model shops which exhibit considerable originality in design and assembly but cannot be said to represent specific types of tree.

Shrubs, hedges, flowering plants and the like are easily contrived from scraps of plastic foam and dependent on the variety, the blossoms can be copied either by snippets of crêpe paper or blobs of process white, touched in when dry with a dab of fluorescent paint. While we are considering general finishes, the rambler rose or Virginia creeper on a cottage wall lends a convincing touch to the scene. The stems can be represented by the florist's accessory sold as 'sea grass' or 'Norwegian moss', the foliage from the Woodland Scenics foam and in the case of ivy

and Virginia creeper, a final spray with hair lacquer will bring a shine to the leaves.

The finishing touch to a convincing model is provided by a suitable backscene and for some reason this seems to present an almost insurmountable obstacle to many enthusiasts. It is possible to buy very good ready-printed scenic sheets from a local model shop, those marketed by one or two West German firms being especially well done. They are enlargements from colour photographs taken in flat perspective and if your model is of a continental prototype, they offer a good solution. With high wooded hills or mountains they are not much help to the modeller of the British scene who is unfortunately not very well catered for. All models, and in particular model railways, unless specifically designed for dioramic presentation with an implied restriction to the viewpoint, require a backscene, preferably drawn in parallel perspective but in any case so arranged, that the effects of perspective resolution to a vanishing point do not detract from the realism of the modelling. An element of 'distance' can be achieved by perspective modelling in which isolated buildings beyond the railway can be constructed to a smaller scale, but it must be done with care.

Porthcurno backscene in water colour.

The photograph on page 86 gives an indication of what can be done by careful selection from suitable coloured pictures culled from calendars or posters. This particular example is a composite of two illustrations from a brochure produced by John Hinde and readily obtainable from W.H. Smith & Son Ltd (The Magnificent South West). The join between the two prints occurs almost immediately above the coupling between the locomotive and the Siphon F and as it occurs in the middle of an open section of seascape, requires special measures to disguise it. The two sections of the scene had the sky portion cut away and were then mounted on artist's water colour board upon which a suitable replacement sky was painted to match in with the prints. The next problem was the water itself. A wash of pale cerulean blue poster colour was made up and painted over the whole of the sea area, the breakers being touched in with process white when the first colour was dry.

In a seascape of this nature the problems of perspective do not have to be considered and on the whole the effect is reasonably satisfactory, the only weakness being the difference in surface texture between the portions of the scene painted in poster or water colour and the slightly glazed finish of the original colour printing.

The backscene illustrated on pages 87 and 89 was prepared in a rather different manner, mainly to avoid any obstrusive joins on a lengthy section of track in open country. The sky was tackled first of all in pastels, which were first powdered by scraping with a penknife, the powder being applied to the wall surface with a pad of cotton wool. The shadow sides of the clouds were put in first by dipping the pad into burnt umber and rubbing briskly where required, varied with a little yellow ochre as the cumulous came into the light. The open sky was indicated by powdered windsor blue at the zenith shading down to a palish green at the horizon.

The result was a very smooth transition from colour to colour with no hard edges and positively no drips. The highlights were the last feature to be treated and were picked out with a soft green eraser, cleaning the rubber frequently on a scrap piece of paper.

The distant landscape was indicated by greens and browns taken down with a little charcoal grey, the finishing touches being applied with various felt tip pens, the white fence in the foreground being indicated in white ink

An oblique view of the backscene – the picture remains in perspective!

applied with a pen.

This entire scene which is over 3ft in length was completed in just over 20 minutes, the secret (if there is one) being not to linger on any specific details but to aim for a clean uncluttered effect. If scene painting is not your forté, this method will probably appeal to you as little time is taken up by the work and the broad treatment does not detract from the detail in the foreground. Furthermore, from whatever angle the scene is viewed, no visual distortion is caused by perspective complications.

If, however, you find you have a taste for this side of the hobby, the type of backscene illustrated in the photographs on pages 90, 91 and 92 will probably be found more interesting. Certainly a little care and patience in drawing out such a view will be more than rewarded by the charm and interest it brings to the layout.

The harbour scenery is based on a number of photographs of Polperro taken on a Cornish holiday. The whole of the built up scene is drawn in what may be loosely termed, parallel perspective. The eaves, ridges, lines of windows, quay walls, and so on are all perfectly level and are in fact drawn with a square in pure elevation. The return gables are drawn in the same way to give depth to the buildings.

Take your time over drawing in the details, working on good quality water colour board taped down to your work top. I cannot pretend that indicating a multiplicity of windows and doors does not become a trifle tedious, but if you find this to be the case, leave the work for a while and do something else, returning to the drawing the following evening. The reflections in the water give considerable visual impact and should be plotted from the base of each cottage with a pair of dividers. Remember that the roofs are falling away from the eye and for this reason will show a diminished reflection. Similarly as the houses climb the cliff, they will show less and less of a reflected image, a point easily checked by setting the dividers to the base of each cottage as it rises on the hill and extending down towards the estuary. By about the second row of buildings, their effect on the water will have ceased.

When the whole of the scene was completed, I lined in the work with waterproof sepia ink before starting the general colouring in water colours. The hillside was painted first, followed by the house roofs, then in turn the eaves shadows, the windows, doors and details of the quays. The rendered surfaces of the walls were mostly left as untouched white paper, but a pale wash of ochre or very light brown was applied here and there for added interest. All the window frames and glazing bars were picked out in white ink when the preceding washes were completely dry.

This particular section of scenery took almost a week of spare time to complete but the effect is pleasing and I consider the time was well spent. You will be surprised how easy the work is if approached in a methodical fashion and it lends an individual quality to your model which cannot be achieved in any other way.

And in conclusion, if perusal of this chapter and of the book as a whole has opened your eyes to the beauty of nature and the interest of man's works in harmony with it, I shall consider my labours have been well rewarded.

The combination of painted backscene, modelled scenery and buildings, and the train in its setting.

Glossary of Architectural Terms

Architrave   The moulded frame round a door or window.

Bargeboard   The sloping timber board which forms the finish to a gable and is commonly fixed to the ends of the purlins when they project through the wall.

Came   The lead strip usually of H section which joins the pieces of glass together in stained glass windows, usually in churches.

Casement   A window which is hinged on one vertical edge and opens like a door. The term is often incorrectly used to describe a complete window.

Corbel   A timber, stone, or iron protrusion from a wall, usually supporting part of the structure or a feature above.

Cornice   The crowning or upper portion of the decorated eaves of Georgian or Regency buildings. It is frequently further enriched with Dentils (see later).

Crenellations   Are loosely described as battlements and describe a parapet which is indented at regular intervals, used as a decorative finish in church work but taken originally from the fortifications of mediaeval castles.

Crocket   A projecting block or spur of stone used to decorate the raking lines of pinnacles, spires and canopies of Gothic churches.

Dentil   Tooth-like blocks of stone or timber set on the underside of a projecting cornice as a form of enrichment. They catch the light in an attractive and interesting manner and throw an intriguing shadow.

Fascia   A vertical face of small projection. A term usually applied to the board above a shop window carrying the name of the proprietor or the vertical board to the eaves of a building to which the rainwater gutter is fixed.

Gable   A triangular shaped wall which is enclosed by the ends or verges of a pitched roof. It is also broadly used to describe the end wall of a building with a pitched roof.

Hip   The junction between two planes of a roof which form an external angle, usually finished with hip tiles or a lead roll. The junction between similar roof planes which form an internal angle is known as a VALLEY.

Oriel   A window corbelled or cantilevered out from the face of a wall as a square or angled bay.

Pediment   In classical or Renaissance architecture, a pediment is a triangular piece of wall, usually set above the cornice. It is frequently enriched with mouldings which echo the treatment of the cornice and often is equipped with dentils (See the Custom House details).

Pilaster   A rectangular projection from the face of a wall in the shape of a pillar but projecting only one sixth of its breadth from the wall. It usually carries a capital and base mouldings like a free standing column.

Pinnacle   A small pointed turret, often enriched with crockets which formed the upper termination of a buttress or was used to add interest to the parapet of a church tower.

Purlin   Horizontal timbers supported by walls giving mid-point support to rafters in a pitched roof.

Quoin   Broadly speaking means the outer corner of a wall or the external angle of a building where two facades meet. Otherwise it refers to the corner stones at the angles of a structure which form an ornamental feature particularly in Georgian architecture.

Ridge   The upper termination of a roof where the two sides meet and terminated with ridge tiles. Always horizontal as distinct from hips which are set on the rake.

Sash   A wooden or metal frame enclosing the separate panes of a window and usually descriptive of the two separate elements of a vertical sash window, where the window opens by sliding the sashes up or down.

Side cheeks   The side walls of a dormer window which is a window set in a sloping roof and so called because it usually gave light to a sleeping apartment. The dormer cheeks were usually finished with sheet lead.

Soffit   The underside of any architectural member. For example the eaves board to a roof where it overhangs the walls is commonly referred to as the soffit board to distinguish it from the fascia.

String Course Is a horizontal projecting moulding either in brick or stone and in Georgian work is often used to break up the facade by giving a degree of horizontal emphasis. At its simplest it consists of a band of two or three courses of brickwork projecting approximately 2¼ in from the main face.

Voussoir   The wedge shaped block of either brick or stone which together form an arch. The central block is often ornamentally carved or projects from the general face and is known as the KEY STONE.

Index